Dear Mummy
A very Happy Christmas 1997.
With much love
Rachel Williams xxx

The Magic of
SAUCERY

Contents

Foreword

Sonia's humility is extraordinary. In the chapter devoted to her in Kit Chapman's book *Great British Chefs*, he states that 'the story of Sonia Stevenson is the story of the most celebrated lady chef of our generation'.

Even after the restaurant which she founded became the first ever to be awarded two stars for cuisine by Egon Ronay on its first entry in his Guide, even after holding the top accolade of three stars for ten years and even after being the first woman ever to be invited into the Michelin three-star kitchens of Maxim's in Paris (and to prepare a dish there for them at that), she is even now always not only ready, but actually happy to learn from anyone.

She was nineteen when we married and, becoming bored with bangers and mash, she asked the Master Butcher at Barkers for a leg of beef. He looked slightly unfocused. 'For how many, madam?' 'Two.' In a totally changed voice he said confidentially, 'You got the wrong cut, ducks!' and Instruction began.

When we abandoned professional music (Sonia was a violinist) – which had originally brought us together, but had proved uneconomic – in view of the reputation she had among our friends, a country restaurant seemed the best answer.

Sonia was very frightened at the idea – she never has realized how marvellous she is – and so we approached our friends at the French hotel from which all our continental adventures started, the Grand Hotel Clement at Ardres, ten miles from Calais. They were very kind and invited us to spend five days in their kitchens to see the discipline, and how and in what order and by whom things were normally done in a professional establishment. Apart from two sensational afternoons with La Mère Brazier three years before, this constituted the only cookery lessons she ever had in her life. Seven days.

So was born the Horn of Plenty in Devon, where one element was a total joy to everyone from the start – Sonia's perfect sauces and gravies, which she always slightly altered to suit the particular preparation they were to accompany: the alterations were ongoing, and the results have always been lovely.

It has always been the actual TASTE from our trips abroad which she was able to recall, rather than simply the appearance, and it has always been the TASTE of everything she prepares that counts. A case of not what it is but how it is done. Not what but how. And on her happy cookery courses, amidst a great deal of laughter, she can manage to teach others to produce those marvellous tastes.

I have been a wonderfully lucky man.

Patrick Stevenson

Introduction

Everyone has to begin somewhere when they enter the jungle of saucemaking; but even a maze has a key and a way out. I hope this book is it!

The Magic of Saucery has been writing itself for years from the inside out. Most people study a subject and it becomes a career, but all my life I seem to have done things the wrong way around. I didn't intend to be a cook, but a violinist. Then I met a hungry orphan who took me to restaurants and showed me what food could really taste like. I married him too – the way to this woman's heart is through her stomach!

I tried to copy the dishes that I tasted in restaurants and, with help and encouragement from chefs and friends, I did.

So we opened our restaurant. Most of the dishes I cooked had no written recipes, but our customers wanted to know how they could copy me in their turn. As I wrote down the recipes for them, I began to find a pattern, a routine, that I was subconsciously following. The Sautéing followed by the Flambéing, followed by the Alcohol or Vinegar Reduction, followed by the Flavouring, followed by the Base, the Simmering and the Finishing.

This routine seemed to be the all-important key. I started to analyse what I was doing and so my learning began, as I questioned the reasons why I would sometimes brown the meats, while at other times I would gently simmer them in a delicious liquid. Even if practice doesn't always make perfect, it certainly gave me time to discover why things are as they are.

It must also be said that, when I began, very many ingredients were not only unobtainable, but unheard of here in the West of England. This made life a lot simpler, and as the years went by I added new ingredients to my dishes, as they became available. However, it was interesting to observe that a high standard of performance was just as achievable with the simple things as with the *embarras de richesse* of ingredients which we have now. As my husband Patrick reminds me continually, 'It's not what it is, but how you use it that counts'.

Anyway, to get back to sauces, other people told me that these were my forte, but that was not what I intended. I was cooking food, and the sauces evolved either as a composite part of the dish, or as a complementary flavouring to a particular meat. In fact I seldom regarded them as sauces – but rather as the necessary background to a stew, or as a simmering medium for a chicken or as a contrasting, acidulated butter to bring out the flavour of a fish.

Occasionally, the sauce itself was a way of showing off a delicious combination of herb flavours and only needed a sympathetic background to support it.

So, too, with fruit coulis – and as an accompaniment to vanilla ices, they take a lot of beating. In this type of cooking, sauces and coulis are not a luxury, but a necessity.

And in the matter of appearance, the colour of each sauce must reflect the depth of its flavour. It is no good having a rich, deep red wine sauce that tastes of cardboard, or a pale cream sauce that takes the skin off your mouth without any warning. The sauce must look as interesting as it tastes.

Salt is always a problem, since it is so much a matter of personal taste. However, once a level of seasoning has been established – in a restaurant, or in a meal – it must be consistent across all the dishes. You can't heavily salt one dish, and lightly salt the next one, to make up for it. Balance is a great virtue – as is moderation.

There is, to my mind, no 'right' consistency for a sauce, but there is always a right consistency for the sauce of a specific dish, and that means they have to be capable of being thinned, thickened, made lighter or heavier as required, and this is simply a matter of technique.

Flavour comes from the ingredients – and the quality of the ingredients is of paramount importance, as is also the judicial selection and mixing of tastes. It's like mixing colours on a palette – too many and the result is a dirty brown. You have to be selective to make a point.

Out of the mass of dishes I have cooked, for this book I have chosen those that need only four bases on which to build a variety of dishes. There are other many other bases, and many more dishes, but the 150 or more in this first book are enough to start with!

Each base is made separately, and since there are only four of them and the cow has made one already with a little help from industry, there are really only three. Sugar Syrup doesn't take long, and mixing eggs and hot butter takes all of 20 seconds, so there is really only *one* you have to worry about, and that will save you *hours* of time in the long run if you make it in advance, in a leisurely fashion, and store it in the freezer. There are certainly some short cuts for the busy, lazy or desperate cook – like buying your stock instead of making it – and the dishes will work if the stock is good enough. However stock-making is not in the least difficult, so I would always recommend making your own.

Having mastered the bases, the fun really begins. The dishes roll out with amazing ease and variety and – with just a change of spice here, or an extra ingredient there, and using a different meat from the one suggested – before long you'll be designing your own dishes, and writing your own recipes and probably opening a restaurant!

I know there are many different ways of achieving the same result, but there are some techniques that are desperately important to my way of cooking, and I would stress just this one.

I always reduce alcohols and vinegars until they become just a few drops of concentrated flavouring. Boiling down a wine makes it lose its alcohol first, and then a host of other smells that would distort and overpower other flavours – they evaporate and disappear, thank goodness. And the essential characteristics of the wine are all that are left behind – and with these I want to perfume my dishes. In the recipes I have said 'reduce until syrupy', as this is the most descriptive way of putting it. And 'syrupy' usually means only two or three tablespoons of liquid.

Finally, no recipe needs to be exact unless it has a chemical reaction that only works one way – like yeast and cake mixtures that go wrong unless precisely measured. Every 'cooking' is a new performance and if you use fresh ingredients this will vary (how acid is a lemon, for instance?) but the standard of cooking won't. Never try to imitate what you did last time. No concert pianist thinks that, because his performance in Swansea was such a success, the result will be the same if he copies it in Birmingham. He has to allow for the difference in acoustics, temperature, the audience and his own temperament, and so he unconsciously adjusts to the occasion.

So with cooking – in this way, you will never become tired of performing. Your feet may ache but the applause makes up for it (or the bank balance maybe). If not, then leave it to others – and give them the applause they deserve.

Sonia Stevenson

egg
SAUCE BASE

TAKING LESS THAN a minute to make, the Egg Sauce Base could not be simpler. It is, in essence, just unsalted butter, thickened with egg.

I once prepared this recipe for a television food programme. The cameraman announced that he had twenty seconds of film left, and did we have a recipe that would take twenty seconds?

Yes I did – and this was it.

It can be made in a liquidizer or food processor, or by hand with an electric or balloon whisk.

One egg yolk, mixed with a teaspoon of water and 125 g/4 oz of hot, melted, unsalted butter produces 150 ml/¼ pint of Egg Sauce Base. Use multiples of these ingredients to produce the appropriate quantities of Egg Sauce Base for the recipes.

Those recipes include some of the most popular dishes at the Horn of Plenty, such as Salmon in Sorrel Sauce on page 29 and Steamed Turbot with Hollandaise Sauce on page 34.

The Egg Sauce Base is in fact a kind of Hollandaise, and when the traditional Hollandaise flavourings of shallots, wine and white wine vinegar are added to the method, you will have what is probably the easiest Hollandaise you've ever made – and the basis of many other delicious sauces.

1 Cut the unsalted butter into small pieces, heat in a saucepan until it starts to boil. It will separate into golden oil and pale buttermilk.

The Egg Sauce Base will take less than a minute to make – in four simple steps. It can be made in a liquidizer or by hand.

LIQUIDIZER METHOD

1 Melt unsalted butter until it starts to boil.

2 Place the water and the egg yolk or yolks in a liquidizer. Blend until pale (about 10 seconds).

3 Add half a ladleful of butter and process.

4 Add the remaining butter, about half a ladle at a time. Wait a few seconds between adding each one – this allows the egg to absorb the butter.

MAKING WITH ELECTRIC OR HAND WHISK

Some people think this method is better, though it is certainly less convenient.

1 Heat unsalted butter until it starts to boil.

2 Place a damp tea towel in a circle on the work surface to steady the bowl.

2 Place the egg yolk or yolks in a liquidizer, add water, and blend until pale. Add half a ladle of melted butter and process until incorporated.

3 Place the yolk or yolks and water in the bowl. Whisk until the mixture becomes slightly frothy.

4 Add a ladleful of butter and whisk hard. Don't add the next until the last has been incorporated.

WHAT CAN GO WRONG?

This is so easy – so what can go wrong? Since it's a two-step method, only two things can go wrong.

1 Heat: if the butter is too hot, it will fry the sauce. Instead of sauce, you get fried egg. Once an egg is cooked, nothing will uncook it.

2 Speed: don't add the butter too fast, or you stop the emulsion forming. Add it little by little. The usual instruction of 'a slow, steady stream' will guarantee disaster. The ingredients will be desperately trying to form an emulsion, while you are drowning it with a continuous stream of butter which it can't absorb. Much better to give it a mouthful to digest, then another – just like feeding a baby!

3 Continue adding the butter, a ladleful at a time, and processing thoroughly for a few seconds between each addition.

4 When all the butter has been incorporated, the Egg Sauce Base will reach this thick, mayonnaise-like consistency.

FIXING MISTAKES

1 When the sauce 'cuts' (that is, it splits into curdled-looking bits), pour the sauce into a jug, rinse out the liquidizer and whizz up another yolk with 1 teaspoon of water. Add the curdled sauce to the beaten egg, a little at a time, beating well between additions. Warm it up a little before you add it to the new egg.

2 Don't ever try to mend a split sauce just by whizzing it harder – no amount of whisking will solve the problem.

SERVING

Use the Egg Sauce Base immediately, or keep warm for up to 30 minutes before serving.

FREEZING

Freeze in small quantities and use in soup recipes, such as the Cream of Tomato Soup (page 16) or the Cream of Lettuce and Bacon Soup (page 19).

TO MAKE A THICKER SAUCE

Add only the clarified butter in the saucepan, leaving all the white buttermilk in the bottom behind. Alternatively, add extra clarified butter.

TO CLARIFY BUTTER

Heat the butter in a saucepan until it froths. Allow to stand for 5 minutes, then skim off the froth. Pour off the clarified butter, and discard the white buttermilk left behind. Clarified butter will not burn as easily as ordinary butter.

QUANTITY GUIDE

IMPORTANT: USE ONLY UNSALTED BUTTER
For 150 ml/¼ pint Egg Sauce Base:
1 egg yolk, 1 teaspoon water, 125 g/4 oz butter
For 300 ml/½ pint Egg Sauce Base:
2 egg yolks, 2 teaspoons water, 250 g/8 oz butter
For 600 ml/1 pint Egg Sauce Base:
4 egg yolks, 4 teaspoons water, 500 g/1 lb butter.

Carrot and Tarragon Soup

50 g/2 oz butter

1 kg/2 lb carrots, sliced

1 onion, chopped

900 ml/1½ pints chicken stock

chopped leaves of
2 sprigs of tarragon

150 ml/¼ pint Egg Sauce Base

salt and freshly
ground black pepper

A well-known soup combination. Add a little Egg Sauce Base and it becomes a velvety cream soup and softens the hard edge of the carrot taste. To prepare this soup in advance, make it as far as marked*, then reheat and add the Egg Sauce Base just before serving.

Heat the butter in a pan, add the carrots and onions and cook, stirring frequently, until they begin to caramelize.

Add the stock, bring to the boil and simmer for about 15 minutes, or until the carrots are tender.

Pour the hot mixture into a liquidizer or food processor, add the tarragon and lots of pepper, and purée until smooth*. Add the Egg Sauce Base, taste and adjust the seasoning. Serve immediately.

Serves 6

Cream of Tomato Soup

2 tablespoons groundnut oil

1 onion, chopped

1 carrot, sliced

1 sprig of thyme

1 bay leaf

6 peppercorns

25 g/1 oz plain flour

800 g/1 lb 10 oz canned
Italian plum tomatoes

600 ml/1 pint light stock

150 ml/¼ pint Egg Sauce Base

1 teaspoon sugar (or to taste)

salt and freshly
ground black pepper

I think this is the nicest way of making a light tasting tomato soup with a real summer flavour. Canned Italian plum tomatoes will give this soup the strongest flavour of the fruit, but if you grow your own tomatoes, you may like to try this recipe using the reddest and ripest of the crop – peel them in the usual way, and add a little tomato purée to beef up the flavour.

Heat the oil in a large pan, add the onion, carrot, thyme, bay leaf and peppercorns, and cook until lightly browned. Sprinkle the flour over and mix well.

Add the tomatoes, pressing them to a pulp with a potato masher. Bring to the boil and thin out with the stock. Cover and simmer for at least 2 hours.

Remove the bay leaf, then pour in batches into a liquidizer or food processor and purée, adding the Egg Sauce Base to the final batch.

Thin out to the required consistency (with water if necessary), then season with the sugar, salt and freshly ground black pepper.

To serve, reheat without boiling, stirring constantly.

Serves 6

Mussel Soup

Egg Sauce Base gives a silky texture to this soup and, although the mussel juices contribute much to the flavour, you will also need a good fish stock for this soup.

To prepare the garnish, clean the leek and cut the tender leaves lengthways, or use a pasta machine, as described below. Set aside.

Heat the butter and water in a large pan, add the fennel, leek, onion, lemon zest and star anise and cook until softened but not coloured. Add the white wine, bring to the boil and reduce until the mixture is slightly syrupy. Add the fish stock, whisk in the *beurre manié*, then simmer for at least 30 minutes. Remove the star anise, strain and reserve the vegetables and stock separately. Purée the vegetables in a food processor or liquidizer.

Wash the mussels as described on page 75. Place them in a large pan, pour in the reserved ladleful of fish stock, and cover tightly. Cook for a few minutes, shaking the pan from time to time, until they open.

As soon as the mussels open, pick them out and, remove and discard the shells. Filter the mussel juice and cooking liquid through muslin to remove the sediment. Return the puréed vegetables and their strained stock to the pan, add the mussel juices, bring to the boil and reduce to about 1.5 litres/2½ pints.

Pour 300 ml/½ pint of the liquid into a liquidizer or food processor, add the Egg Sauce Base and purée until smooth. Whisk this mixture back into the remaining liquid. Taste and adjust the seasoning.

Divide the mussels between heated soup plates, ladle the soup over them and garnish with strips of leek. Serve with good crusty bread to mop up the juices.

Serves 6

50 g/2 oz butter

150 ml/1/4 pint water

1 bulb of fennel, sliced

1 medium leek, sliced

1 onion, sliced

grated zest of 1 lemon

2 star anise

300 ml/½ pint white wine

1.8 litres/3 pints fish stock
(reserve 1 ladleful for
cooking the mussels)

beurre manié made with
50 g/2 oz flour mixed
with 75 g/3 oz butter

36 fresh mussels

150 ml/¼ pint Egg Sauce Base

salt and lots of freshly
ground black pepper

1 leek, to garnish (see below)

Note:

LEEK GARNISH

Split and thoroughly rinse the leek, then feed lengthways through a pasta machine, using the very fine trenette cutter. This will produce very fine strips of leek. Blanch and drain before using for garnish.

Creamy Vichyssoise

500 g/1 lb leeks,
white part only

50 g/2 oz butter

2 onions, sliced

500 g/1 lb floury
potatoes, sliced

1.5 litres/2½ pints light stock

150 ml/¼ pint Egg Sauce Base

150 ml/¼ pint milk
(optional)

salt and freshly
ground black pepper

3 tablespoons chopped
fresh chives, to garnish

When this soup is made with Egg Sauce Base, it is beautifully creamy, yet contains no cream and so is very light. Use big, floury potatoes, such as King Edwards or the ones sold as jacket potatoes. You could also substitute a little ham water, if you have it on hand, for some of the light stock, to give a slightly different flavour.

Slit the leeks in half lengthways and wash out all the mud and dirt, changing the water frequently.

Heat the butter in a large pan, add the leeks and onions and cook gently for 5 minutes until softened but not coloured. Add the potatoes and stock, bring to the boil and simmer for 20 minutes or until the potatoes are soft.

Purée in batches in a liquidizer or food processor, adding the Egg Sauce Base to the last batch and thinning out with milk if necessary. Add freshly ground black pepper, taste and adjust the seasoning.

Serve very cold, sprinkled with the chopped chives.

Serves 6

Lentil and Bacon Soup

50 g/2 oz butter

1 carrot, sliced

3 rashers rindless, smoked
streaky bacon, chopped

1 medium onion, chopped

175 g/6 oz lentils, well rinsed

2 teaspoons curry paste

2 teaspoons ground cumin

1.8 litres/3 pints stock

150 ml/¼ pint Egg Sauce Base

salt and freshly
ground black pepper

A warming, comforting soup that's also quick to make. You could use Egyptian or red lentils, or even leftover dhaal from a curry. Use chicken, ham or beef stock for good flavour, and mild or medium curry paste, according to taste.

Heat the butter in a pan and fry the carrot, bacon and onion until they begin to brown. Add the lentils and fry for a further 2 minutes. Add the curry paste and ground cumin and cook for 2 minutes more.

Cover with the stock and simmer until the lentils are tender, about 30 minutes. Pour the mixture, in batches, into a liquidizer or food processor and purée until smooth, adding the Egg Sauce Base to the final batch.

Pour into a saucepan, mix well and reheat without boiling. Taste and adjust the seasoning, then serve.

Serves 6

Cream of Lettuce and Bacon Soup

This is a very useful recipe for using the outer leaves of lettuce, reserving the heart for salad. Don't cook it for longer than about five minutes, or you will lose the beautiful green colour.

If you prefer a strong bacon flavour, use a stock made from a ham bone, but this chicken stock with bacon added gives a nice balance. If you like your soup very rich and creamy, increase the quantity of Egg Sauce Base – to as much as 300 ml/½ pint.

Place the butter and bacon in a pan and cook gently until softened but not coloured. Add the lettuce leaves and cook gently until fully limp.

Add 600 ml/1 pint of stock, bring to the boil and simmer for about 5 minutes. Pour into a liquidizer or food processor and blend at full speed until as fine as possible. Add a little stock, followed by the Egg Sauce Base. Strain through a colander into the rinsed pan to get rid of coarse lettuce fibres and bacon lumps.

Add the remaining stock, reheat without boiling, taste and adjust the seasoning, and serve, sprinkled with the chopped fresh herbs.

Serves 6

50 g/2 oz butter

3 rashers streaky bacon, chopped

the tough outer leaves of 3 large, soft-leafed lettuces (not Cos or iceberg)

1.5 litres/2½ pints hot chicken or ham stock

150 ml/¼ pint Egg Sauce Base

salt and freshly ground black pepper

3 tablespoons chopped, fresh, flat leaf parsley or chives, to garnish

Hollandaise Sauce

This is my own, easy version of Hollandaise Sauce. It is one of the most versatile of sauces – particularly good with fish and vegetables, such as asparagus and salsify, and other delicate flavours.

Heat the butter and peppercorns in a small pan, add the shallots and cook until softened but not coloured. Add the vinegar and wine, bring to the boil and reduce until syrupy. Add the water and boil hard for a few minutes to draw the vinegar flavouring out of the shallots.

Strain through a fine sieve, squeezing the shallots against the sides to extract all the flavour. Discard the strained solids.

Bring the liquid to the boil and reduce to an emulsion – about 2 tablespoons – then add to the Egg Sauce Base. Taste and adjust the seasoning and serve.

Serves 6

50 g/2 oz butter

10 black peppercorns, lightly crushed

2 shallots, chopped

300 ml/½ pint white wine vinegar

150 ml/¼ pint white wine

150 ml/¼ pint water

600 ml/1 pint Egg Sauce Base

salt

Brussels Sprout Tarts with Lemon Butter Sauce

melted butter for
oiling and brushing

6 sheets filo pastry,
cut into 30 squares of
15 cm/6 inches

125 ml/4 fl oz milk

50 g/2 oz fresh
white breadcrumbs

1 kg/2 lb young
Brussels sprouts

50 g/2 oz butter

2 egg yolks

¼ teaspoon grated nutmeg

12 chestnuts

150 ml/¼ pint milk

300 ml/½ pint Egg Sauce Base

juice of 1 lemon

salt and freshly
ground black pepper

Sprouts can be rather strong in taste, but this lemony sauce actually needs a distinctively flavoured dish to go with it. It makes a fine first course and, without the pastry, a delicious accompaniment to meat.

Brush 6 individual 10 cm/4 inch tins with melted butter and then make 6 pastry bases by laying 5 layers of filo pastry in each. Brush each layer with melted butter, before placing it fanways around the tin. When they are all in place, fold over the pointed ends to make a firm border, or leave frilled, as in the photograph.

Prick the base with a fork, and brush over a final coating of melted butter. Bake in a preheated oven at 220°C (425°F) Gas Mark 7 for about 7–8 minutes, or until crisp and browned. Remove from the oven, allow to cool, then carefully remove from the tins.

Use the same or similar tins to bake the filling, buttering them well before use. To make the filling, first heat the milk in a small pan, then add the breadcrumbs and set aside to rest.

Cook the sprouts in boiling salted water until just tender. Refresh under the cold tap, then place in a cloth and squeeze out all the water. Chop coarsely, place in a liquidizer or food processor, add the butter and egg yolks and purée until smooth. Turn into a bowl and stir in the milk and breadcrumb mixture. Season with salt, freshly ground black pepper and lots of nutmeg.

Fill the buttered tins with the mixture and stand them in a *bain-marie* filled with water to half way up their sides. Cook very gently for about 20–25 minutes.

Meanwhile, boil the chestnuts for 5 minutes to soften the shells. Peel, place the kernels in a pan, cover with milk, bring to the boil and simmer until soft. Cut them into pieces and keep in the milk until required. When ready to use, reheat and drain off the milk.

Turn the sprout mixture out of the tins and lift carefully into the pastry cases, cooked side up, then add the chestnut pieces. Add salt, and lemon juice to taste, to the warm Egg Sauce Base.

To serve, place the filled tarts on heated starter plates, and spoon the sauce over.

Serves 6

Smoked Haddock and Cucumber with Hollandaise

1 kg/2 lb smoked haddock

about 300 ml/½ pint milk,
or to cover

2 cucumbers

2 hard-boiled eggs

300 ml/½ pint Hollandaise
Sauce, made with Egg
Sauce Base (see page 19)

lemon juice,
to taste (optional)

salt and freshly
ground black pepper

1 tablespoon chopped fresh
flat leaf parsley, to garnish

Properly smoked haddock (not the painted variety) is one of the most British of flavours. Add the gentle silkiness of the Egg Sauce Base – flavoured with lemon juice if preferred – and you have a perfect hot summer starter or light luncheon dish.

Another interesting variation – grate a little fresh ginger into the butter when you make the base.

Place the haddock in a pan, cover with milk and simmer until done.

Cut the ends off the cucumbers and slice them in half lengthways, peel and remove the seeds. Slice into 2.5 cm/1 inch lengths and then simmer for 10 minutes in boiling salted water.

Roughly chop the haddock and eggs and season with freshly ground black pepper. Taste and add salt only if necessary. Place in an oval gratin dish with the drained pieces of cucumber. Add a squeeze of lemon juice, if using, to the Hollandaise Sauce, then pour over the fish, and garnish with the chopped parsley.

Serves 6

Peas with Fennel Sauce

discarded leaves and stalks from
2-4 bulbs of fennel, chopped

50 g/2 oz butter

300 ml/½ pint water

50 ml/2 fl oz Egg Sauce Base

375 g/12 oz cooked green peas
(about 1.23 kg/2½ lb in the pod)

A delicious way to the trimmings and outer leaves of fennel bulbs used in other dishes. This recipe is good to serve with fish, roasted or grilled meats. Use leftover or frozen Egg Sauce Base – the thawed base will split, but the water will make it emulsify again.

Heat the butter and water in a non-stick pan, cover and braise the pieces of fennel until softened. Place in a liquidizer or food processor, purée, then push through a sieve or mouli. Return the purée to the pan and cook until most of the moisture has evaporated.

Remove from the heat, dip the base of the hot pan into cold water, and stir in the Egg Sauce Base. Mix well, then add this sauce to the freshly cooked peas.

Serves 6

Broccoli 'Asparagus' with Tarragon and Tomato Sauce

Broccoli stalks are commonly known as the 'poor man's asparagus'. They certainly fulfil the same purpose but they are nice enough to have a place of their own as a first course. Choose very fresh broccoli with long stalks, and serve the florets with another dish. Chard stalks can be served in the same way, but only as an accompaniment to meat or fish, as their flavour is too earthy to stand alone.

Using a vegetable peeler, strip the tough outsides off the broccoli stalks and cut the tender centres into asparagus-sized batons. Cook in boiling salted water until tender, then drain and keep warm.

   Place the butter, vinegar and shallot in a saucepan, bring to the boil and reduce to about 1 teaspoon. (Take care not to burn it.) Stir in the cream, tomato purée, paprika, meat glaze, if using, and tarragon. Bring to the boil, add the tomato, warm, then add the Egg Sauce Base. Place the broccoli on heated plates, and spoon the sauce over.

Serves 6

1 kg/2 lb broccoli stalks

25 g/1 oz butter

150 ml/¼ pint tarragon vinegar

1 shallot, chopped

1 tablespoon single cream

1 teaspoon tomato purée

1 teaspoon paprika

1 teaspoon meat glaze (optional)

1 tablespoon
chopped fresh tarragon

1 tomato, skinned,
deseeded and diced

300 ml/½ pint Egg Sauce Base,
warmed

Purée of Swedes

This recipe is for the rich, yellow variety of swede – the kind called 'neeps' in Scotland and rutabaga in America and Europe. The taste can be very strong, but when muted with the Egg Sauce Base, it makes a gorgeous purée. Serve this recipe in winter with dishes such as pheasant and guinea fowl – it's perfect for mopping up gravy.

Boil the swede in plenty of salted water until it can be pierced through with a knife. Drain off the water and leave the swede in a large metal colander and allow it to steam dry.

   Place the swede and the Egg Sauce Base in a liquidizer or food processor, and purée until smooth. Add plenty of freshly ground black pepper, taste and adjust the seasoning and serve hot.

Serves 6

1 large swede, about
1.25 kg/2½ lb, peeled and sliced

150 ml/¼ pint Egg Sauce Base

salt and lots of freshly
ground black pepper

24

Courgette and Chicken Dariole with Tarragon Sauce

3 tablespoons groundnut oil

500 g/1 lb courgettes

75 g/3 oz chicken breast,
with all skin, bone
and sinews removed

2 egg yolks

50 ml/2 fl oz milk

75 ml/3 fl oz whipping cream

salt and freshly
ground black pepper

For the sauce:
50 ml/2 fl oz whipping cream

300 ml/½ pint Egg Sauce Base

1 tablespoon chopped
fresh tarragon leaves

sprigs of watercress,
to garnish

This is an excellent starter – it can be reheated gently or assembled beforehand and cooked when needed. Although the technique is the same as for the Leek Mousse on page 54, it is less creamy in texture. Leave in some chunky bits of courgette or add a few chopped water chestnuts for extra crunchiness.

Use less oil in this recipe if you like – it's only there to provide a buffer between the pan and the courgettes.

Don't be alarmed when you see the amount of liquid that comes out of the courgettes. If you get impatient, you can always pour some off, but you will lose some of the flavour if you do.

Heat 2 tablespoons of the oil in a non-stick pan. Grate the unpeeled courgettes or cut them up roughly in a food processor, then turn out into the pan, and cook, pressing them down with a potato masher to squeeze out and boil off as much water as possible – you should have 200 ml/7 fl oz of pulp. Set aside to cool.

Place the chicken and egg yolks in a liquidizer or food processor, purée until smooth. Lightly blend in the courgettes, milk and cream but do not purée. Turn out into a bowl. Taste and add salt and lots of freshly ground black pepper.

Brush 6 dariole moulds or small bowls with the remaining oil, spoon in the mixture and cook in a preheated oven at 150°C (300°F) Gas Mark 2 for about 30 minutes, or until set. Do not allow to rise – which it will if the oven is too hot.

To make the sauce, pour the cream into a pan and simmer until it is slightly thickened, as described in Step 2 on page 52. Whisk in the Egg Sauce Base, then add the chopped fresh tarragon.

To serve, turn out the darioles on to heated starter plates, spoon the sauce beside and garnish with sprigs of watercress.

Serves 6

Fillet of Trout with Broccoli and Mustard Stuffing

Check the fish, even if your fishmonger has filleted it, and remove every single bone. There are excellent fish tweezers on the market but even ordinary ones work quite well.

To make the stuffing, cook the broccoli in boiling salted water until tender, then refresh under cold water. Place the shallot, vinegar and butter in a saucepan and simmer gently until syrupy. Add the flour, then stir in the milk to make a white sauce. Cook for a few minutes, then add the mustard.

Reserve some broccoli for garnish, and then put the remainder in a liquidizer or food processor. Add the white sauce, eggs, egg yolks and seasoning, then purée until smooth. Season well.

Line a Swiss roll tin with foil, then pour in the mixture and cook in a preheated oven at 160°C (325°F) Gas Mark 3 for about 25 minutes until set. Do not allow it to rise and become a soufflé, or the texture will be spoiled. Remove from the oven, leave to cool, then chill.

Remove all the bones from the fillets, turn them over and season. Cut a square of cold stuffing one-third the length of the fish and place in the middle of each fillet. Fold over the ends of the fillet to make an open parcel and turn over to place the join underneath. Refrigerate until needed. (You can prepare the dish in advance up to this point.)

To make the sauce, place the shallots, butter and vinegar in a pan and simmer until syrupy. Add the water and bring to the boil. Strain the mixture, pushing through as much flavour as possible. Return to the boil and reduce to 1 tablespoon. Stir in the Egg Sauce Base, cream and seasoning. Set aside and keep warm.

To cook the fish, dust both sides with the seasoned flour, heat the butter in a large pan and fry the fish parcels, turning them once, until lightly browned. Place the fish on heated dinner plates, pour the sauce around, garnish with the reserved broccoli and keep warm. If you would like to shine up the fish with a black butter sauce, add vinegar to the pan, bring to the boil and reduce until the foam subsides and the kick has almost disappeared from the flavour. Taste and adjust the seasoning, then pour over the fish and sauce. Serve immediately.

Serves 6

6 trout, filleted and skinned, about 375 g/12 oz each

1 tablespoon seasoned flour

125–175 g/4–6 oz butter

75 ml/3 fl oz white wine vinegar (optional)

salt and freshly ground black pepper

For the stuffing:
750 g/1½ lb broccoli

1 shallot, chopped

300 ml/½ pint white wine vinegar

50 g/2 oz butter

25 g/1 oz flour

250 ml/8 fl oz milk

4 teaspoons Dijon mustard

2 eggs and 2 egg yolks

For the sauce:
2 shallots, chopped

50 g/2 oz butter

300 ml/½ pint white wine vinegar

150 ml/¼ pint water

250 ml/8 fl oz Egg Sauce Base

125 ml/4 fl oz whipping 27cream

Eggs on Pastry with Shellfish in Two Sauces

This is my husband's favourite recipe – basically an Eggs Benedict, with shellfish in a vermouth cream sauce instead of the ham. The eggs can be poached in advance and slipped into cooler water to stop them cooking. Drain and dry them before placing on the pastry case.

Line 6 individual tartlet tins with a round of puff pastry. Cook in a preheated oven, 220°C (425°F) Gas Mark 7 for about 15 minutes, or until the pastry is puffed and golden.

To achieve a very thin base, remove the top half of the pastry and any soft insides, and discard. Return the remaining thin base to the oven to dry out (being careful not to burn it), then turn out on to a rack to cool. Alternatively, prick the pastry base and cook, sandwiched between two tartlet tins.

To make the vermouth sauce, heat the butter in a saucepan, add the shallots and cook until softened but not coloured. Add the vermouth, bring to the boil and reduce to a buttery syrup. Add the flour and mix thoroughly. Whisk in the cream, bring to the boil and simmer for about 5 minutes to release the flavours.

Add the cheeses, mustard, nutmeg and salt and pepper to taste. Bring to the boil, cover and set aside.

Poach the eggs in salted water if you have not already done so (see introduction). Add a little salt and a squeeze of lemon juice to the warm Egg Sauce Base.

To serve, add the prawns to the vermouth sauce, and reheat without allowing it to boil or you will toughen the prawns. Return the pastry cases to the oven to reheat.

To reheat the Egg Sauce Base, place on the heat for 5 seconds. Lift off and whisk the heat in – do this a couple of times to bring the sauce up to serving temperature. (Do not put into a double boiler to reheat, or you will cook the egg and split the sauce.)

Divide the prawn mixture between the 6 pastry cases. Drain and place the poached eggs on top. Spoon the Egg Sauce Base over the top and serve, garnished with sprigs of chervil, salmon or lobster roe, and caviar, as you prefer.

Serves 6

6 rounds of puff pastry, 12 cm/5 inches in diameter

6 eggs

1 tablespoon lemon juice

300 ml/½ pint Egg Sauce Base, warmed

6 cooked tiger prawns or 1 lobster

salt and freshly ground black pepper

For the vermouth sauce:
50 g/2 oz butter

2 shallots, chopped

300 ml/½ pint white vermouth

2 teaspoons flour

300 ml/½ pint whipping cream

15 g/½ oz Gruyère cheese, grated

15 g/½ oz Parmesan cheese, grated

2 teaspoons Dijon mustard

¼ teaspoon nutmeg

To garnish (optional):
sprigs of chervil

salmon or lobster roe, and caviar

Sea Bass with Mustard Sauce

**6 filleted portions of sea bass,
about 175–250 g/6–8 oz each
(about 1 large fish)**

50 g/2 oz seasoned flour

**salt and freshly
ground black pepper**

**3 tablespoons chopped fresh
flat leaf parsley, to garnish**

For the mustard sauce:
**Cream Sauce Base, made with
125 ml/4 fl oz whipping cream**

300 ml/½ pint Egg Sauce Base

25 g/1 oz melted butter

1 tablespoon tarragon mustard

Sea bass has flesh that mops up moisture, so is ideal for serving with butter sauces. It can be steamed – but never poached, or it will become waterlogged.

However, nothing brings out the deep taste of this wonderful fish like roasting, as in this recipe. It was certainly one of the greatest favourites at the Horn, many preferring it to salmon.

The bigger the fish the better – a 3.5 kg/7 lb sea bass is perfect, because the fillets are really thick and meaty. Take care not to over-cook it, or it will become dry and cottonwooly very quickly.

To make the Cream Sauce Base, simmer the cream in a small frying pan until it begins to fry and turn a nutty brown *beurre noisette*, as in Step 6, page 53.

Make the Egg Sauce Base as on page 14, add the melted butter, then beat in the mustard and the *beurre noisette*. Taste, adjust the seasoning and put aside to keep warm.

Dust the fish fillets with seasoned flour and lay them, skin-side up, on a very hot, well-buttered baking sheet. Cook in a preheated oven at 230°C (450°F) Gas Mark 8 for about 8 minutes, or until the skin can be easily removed. Remove from the oven and peel off the skin.

Place the fish fillets, brown side up, on heated dinner plates. Pour the sauce beside the fish and run a line of chopped fresh parsley between the fish and the sauce.

Serves 6

Alternatively:
PAN-FRIED FISH
WITH A GREEN
PEPPERCORN SAUCE
Substitute salmon, grey
mullet, haddock or halibut
for the sea bass. Pan-fry in
butter and serve with the
sauce, adding 1 tablespoon
bottled green or pink
peppercorns, drained
and crushed, as well
as the mustard.

Salmon in Sorrel Sauce

This splendid sauce – redolent of the hedgerows where dock leaves sometimes masquerade as sorrel – was instrumental in making the reputation of the Horn of Plenty in our earliest days.

When sorrel is in season, gather large amounts of fresh leaves, wash them, drain and cook in a generous amount of butter. Chill and divide into conveniently sized portions. Keep well wrapped in the deep freezer for use in sauces or soups.

To my mind, this recipe is the best way of cooking a salmon cutlet of top quality and flavour, and serving it in early summer with the sorrel sauce is one of those seasonal revelations. (Don't use any lemon juice for seasoning – it absolutely ruins the taste.)

Bring a large pan or fish kettle of salted water to the boil, then slip in the salmon cutlets. Remove the pan from the heat immediately and set aside in a warm place for about 8 minutes.

Remove the fish to a heated plate, slip off the skin and carefully remove the bones. Keep warm.

To make the sauce, wash the sorrel leaves and shake off most of the moisture. Melt the butter in a large pan and add the sorrel, which will instantly turn khaki-coloured. If not, it isn't sorrel and anything bright green is a foreign body and must be removed.

Make the Egg Sauce Base in a liquidizer, according to the method on page 14, then add the sorrel and butter, and salt to taste, then purée until smooth.

Serves 6

6 salmon cutlets, about 200 g/7 oz each

For the sorrel sauce:
a large handful of fresh sorrel leaves

50 g/2 oz butter

300–450 ml/½–¾ pint Egg Sauce Base, warmed

salt

Note:
SORREL
If you have a garden, it is worthwhile growing a large patch of sorrel for use in sauces or soups. It propagates easily from seed. Otherwise the wild variety is to be found in the autumn and early winter in large clumps of tender leaves at the roadside (but don't pick them from the polluted verges of a busy road – choose a little-frequented country lane instead). Another point worth making – sorrel is milder in spring, so you will need more leaves early in the season to make up the intensity of flavour.

Baked Sea Trout with Champagne Sauce

1 sea trout,
about 2–3 kg/4–5 lb

melted butter, for brushing

salt and freshly
ground black pepper

sprigs of dill or bronze
fennel, to garnish

For the sauce:
1 cucumber

50 g/2 oz butter

2 shallots, chopped

450 ml/¾ pint Champagne

450 ml/¾ pint fish stock

175 ml/6 fl oz whipping cream

450 ml/¾ pint Egg Sauce Base

1 tablespoon chopped dill
or bronze fennel

Sea trout is at its peak in July. It is so delicate, both in texture and flavour, that it is best to cook it whole in its own juices and not to add extra flavour. Champagne is traditionally the wine of celebration (especially pink) but any reasonably delicate white wine will do just as well. If you want to serve it cold at a summer luncheon, brush it with groundnut oil rather than butter (butter will congeal into lumps and look unattractive). The sauce is good hot or cold, but will probably need thinning with water if serving cold.

Brush the fish inside and out with melted butter and sprinkle salt inside the cavity. Wrap in foil and place on a baking sheet. Cook in a preheated oven at 160°C (325°F) Gas Mark 3 for about 45 minutes.

Check inside the sea trout, beside the backbone, to see whether it is cooked sufficiently (a little rare is a good thing).

To make the sauce, peel the cucumber and cut it lengthways into 8 pieces. Remove the seeds, cut each piece into 2.5 cm/1 inch sections and simmer in salted water for 5 minutes. Drain and keep warm.

Heat the butter in a pan, and cook the shallots until softened but not coloured. Add the Champagne, bring to the boil and reduce until syrupy. Pour in the stock and cream, and simmer until reduced to about 450 ml/¾ pint. Add the Egg Sauce Base and whisk vigorously. Taste, adjust the seasoning, then set aside to keep warm.

Unwrap the fish and drain off any liquid so that it can be reduced and added to the sauce later. Peel off the skin, leaving the head intact, and carefully turn the fish over on to a heated serving dish. Remove the skin from the head, plugging the eye socket with a little parsley. Brush over the fish with melted butter.

Pour the drained liquid from the cooked fish into a pan and reduce to about 1 tablespoon. Add to the sauce and fold in the cucumber and chopped dill or fennel, pour it around the fish, or serve separately in a sauceboat. Garnish with sprigs of dill or fennel.

Serves 6

Poached John Dory on Savoury Spinach

John Dory has snow-white, firm-textured flesh which falls into very conveniently sized fillets, three to a side. You can adapt this recipe for small trout – or indeed any firm-fleshed fish.

The texture will be much nicer if you cook the fish on the bone, rather than filleting it before poaching.

Remove the head of the fish and, using scissors, trim the fins all round, removing all the spikes.

Heat the butter in a frying pan, add the shallots and cook gently until softened but not coloured. Add a little salt and lots of freshly ground black pepper, pour in the wine, bring to the boil and reduce until syrupy.

Replace the evaporated liquid with the hot fish stock or water. Lay the fish in an ovenproof dish and pour in the contents of the frying pan. Cover, place in the oven, then turn the oven on to 200°C (400°F) Gas Mark 6. Do not allow it to boil, but bring the temperature of the fish up to about 90°C – just enough to set the flesh. When set (about 8 minutes), remove from the oven and allow to cool a little.

Meanwhile heat the butter for the spinach in the frying pan, add the spinach and herbs and simmer for a few minutes until cooked. Chop the mixture and press out the excess liquid. Season with nutmeg and salt and return it to the pan.

Carefully lift the fish out on to a large dish. Pour the liquid through a strainer into a pan and boil until reduced to 300 ml/½ pint. Beat in the Egg Sauce Base, keep warm.

Remove the skin from the fish and discard. Reheat the spinach and place on heated dinner plates. Remove the fillets from the fish and arrange them on the spinach, pour the sauce around and over, and sprinkle with toasted sesame seeds.

Serves 6

3 large John Dory, to serve 6

150 g/5 oz butter

3 shallots, chopped

300 ml/½ pint
medium white wine

about 450 ml/¾ pint
fish stock or water

salt and freshly
ground black pepper

toasted sesame seeds,
to garnish

For the spinach:
75 g/3 oz butter

250 g/8 oz spinach leaves, with
any hard stalks removed

1 tablespoon fresh
tarragon leaves

1 tablespoon fresh
flat leaf parsley leaves

6 fresh sage leaves

¼ teaspoon grated nutmeg

150 ml/¼ pint Egg Sauce Base

salt and lots of freshly
ground black pepper

32

Smoked Haddock Kedgeree

175 g/6 oz long-grain rice

500 g/1 lb smoked
haddock fillets

150 ml/¼ pint milk

150 ml/¼ pint Egg Sauce Base

4 hard-boiled eggs, chopped

salt and freshly
ground black pepper

Alternatively:
RICE PUDDING WITH
TAMARILLO COULIS

For the Tamarillo Coulis,
roughly chop 6 tamarillos and
poach in 150 ml/¼ pint Sugar
Sauce Base (page 156) until
soft. Press through a sieve and
set aside. For the Rice
Pudding, simmer 75 g/3 oz
Carolina or pudding rice in
900 ml/1½ pints milk with
40 g/1½ oz sugar in a
non-stick pan for 40 minutes,
stirring from time to time,
until done. Most of the liquid
should be absorbed. Cool a
little, then add 150 ml/¼ pint
Egg Sauce Base. Brush 6 coffee
cups or dariole moulds with
oil, fill with the mixture, then
chill. To serve, turn out and
spoon the Tamarillo Sauce
around, and decorate with
poached, sliced tamarillos.

A truly gorgeous Sunday breakfast dish, and one of the greatest of traditional British recipes.

It is ostensibly the product of the Raj. However, it was probably invented by the Irish since it bears no resemblance at all to the Indian Khichree, which in any case contains neither fish nor egg.

The recipe also produces an interesting and unusual variation, based on a traditional Danish Christmas dish – which will change all your preconceptions about rice puddings. In Denmark, crumbled, blanched almonds would be mixed through the rice, while a single, whole almond would take the place of our sixpence-in-the-pudding. You could also stir through some chopped glacé fruits.

The little rice puddings are delicious served with Caramel Sauce (page 168) and spectacular with Tamarillo Sauce and sliced, poached tamarillos, as illustrated below.

Boil or steam the rice using your usual method. Poach the fish in the milk, then strain. Keep the liquid for making a smoked cream sauce – perhaps for scallops, as in the recipe for Scallop Quenelles in Smoked Butter Sauce on page 73.

Flake the fish and mix with the cooked rice. Bind with the Egg Sauce Base and some of the chopped egg, keeping some for garnish. Taste and adjust the seasoning.

Spoon out on to a heated serving dish and sprinkle with chopped egg.
Serves 6

Steamed Turbot with Hollandaise Sauce

6 fillets of turbot, about
175-200 g/6-7 oz each

175 g/6 oz butter

salt and freshly
ground black pepper

For the sauce:
50 g/2 oz butter

10 black peppercorns,
lightly crushed

2 shallots, chopped

300 ml/½ pint
white wine vinegar

150 ml/¼ pint white wine

150 ml/¼ pint water

600 ml/1 pint Egg Sauce Base

A classic dish and a perfect combination – although, indeed, almost any fillets (plaice, brill, John Dory, even Greenland halibut) when prepared this way, show their best flavour.

Food used to be cooked 'en papillote' in packets of greaseproof paper in the oven but, these days, foil is most often used. Certainly, you could never steam paper 'papillotes', or you would end up with some very soggy wrappings!

To cook the fish, generously butter 6 sheets of aluminium foil. Season the fish with salt and freshly ground black pepper, and fold the fillets in half if they are long. Wrap foil securely around each fillet of fish so no juices can escape. Place the parcel over boiling water and steam for 10–15 minutes, according to size. Open the parcel over a sieve with a bowl underneath to catch any juices. Pour these into a pan and reduce to an emulsion to add to the sauce later.

To make the sauce, heat the butter and crushed peppercorns in a small pan, add the shallots and cook until softened but not coloured. Add the vinegar and wine, bring to the boil and reduce until syrupy. Add the water and boil vigorously for a few minutes to draw the reduced vinegar flavouring out of the shallots.

Strain through a fine sieve, squeezing the shallots against the sides to extract all the flavour. Discard the strained solids.

Bring the liquid to the boil and reduce to an emulsion (about 2 tablespoons). Add this, together with the emulsified fish juices, to the Egg Sauce Base. Taste and adjust the seasoning.

To serve, place 1 fillet on each of 6 heated dinner plates and pour the sauce either around the fish or serve separately in a sauceboat.
Serves 6

Mussels and Bacon on a Skewer with Béarnaise Sauce

Béarnaise Sauce is best known as an accompaniment for grilled steaks. I feel it shows to just as great an advantage in this recipe – with mussels and bacon threaded on to a skewer, then covered with breadcrumbs and deep-fried, or drizzled with a little oil or melted butter and grilled or baked in the oven. Serve one skewer per person as a starter, or two as a main course for lunch. For a drinks party, make smaller versions on cocktail sticks to dip into a bowl of sauce. If using wooden skewers, soak them in water for 30 minutes first.

To make the sauce, place the vinegar, butter, peppercorns, shallots and the dried tarragon and half the fresh tarragon leaves in a non-metal or stainless steel saucepan, bring to the boil and simmer until syrupy.

Pour in the measured water and boil fiercely for several minutes. Strain the mixture through a fine sieve into another pan, pressing the shallots against the side to extract all the flavour, but leaving the fibrous material behind. Bring to the boil and reduce to 2 tablespoons. Add the Egg Sauce Base to the concentrated liquid, taste and adjust the seasoning, then add the remaining chopped fresh tarragon.

To prepare the skewers, first clean the mussels as described on page 75, place them in a large pan with 300 ml/½ pint of water, bring to the boil and steam for a minute or so, shaking the pan a couple of times until the mussels open (remove them as they do – do not overcook). Drain and reserve the cooking liquid for another use.

Remove the mussels from their shells and pull off any beards. Cut each bacon rasher into about 6 pieces, double the size of 1 mussel. Fold in half and slide on to a skewer, followed by 2 mussels. Repeat until each skewer has 6 mussels, and ends with a folded piece of bacon. Press the mussels and bacon together.

Dip the loaded skewer first in beaten egg, then in breadcrumbs, pressing on the crumbs to form a good coating. Deep-fry the skewers in groundnut oil and drain on absorbent paper, or drizzle with olive oil and grill or bake in the oven at 220°C (425°F) Gas Mark 7 until done. Remove the skewers, if preferred, and serve with the sauce.

Serves 6

about 1 kg/2 lb/6 pints
fresh mussels

15 rashers streaky bacon

2 eggs, beaten

about 125 g/4 oz
fresh breadcrumbs

groundnut oil, for frying

For the sauce:
300 ml/½ pint
tarragon vinegar

50 g/2 oz butter

10 whole black
peppercorns, crushed

3 shallots, finely chopped

1 teaspoon dried tarragon and
2 tablespoons chopped
fresh tarragon leaves

175 ml/6 fl oz water

300 ml/½ pint Egg Sauce Base

salt and freshly
ground black pepper

Timbale of Rice and Shellfish

1 small cooked crab

75 g/3 oz butter

3 shallots, chopped

150 ml/¼ pint white wine

1 teaspoon Pernod

300 ml/½ pint fish stock

12 whole black peppercorns

300 ml/½ pint water

about 300 g/10 oz
raw king prawns

250 g/8 oz long-grain rice

10 strands saffron

150 ml/¼ pint Egg Sauce Base

3 tablespoons
grated Parmesan cheese

salt and freshly
ground black pepper

To garnish:
sprigs of watercress

3 large tomatoes,
skinned, deseeded and diced

1 tablespoon snipped fresh
chives, or more, to taste

Cooked mussels or shrimps can be added to this dish, as well as pieces of a firm fish, such as monkfish, that won't break up. The result is a creamy hot risotto.

Break off the crab claws and put them aside to remove the meat later. Open the crab and discard the stomach and 'dead men's fingers'. Chop up the rest of the crab, shell and all.

Heat 50 g/2 oz of the butter in a pan, add the shallots and cook until softened but not coloured. Add the wine and Pernod, bring to the boil and reduce until syrupy. Add the fish stock, peppercorns and chopped crab shell.

Bring the water to the boil in a separate pan, drop in the prawns, reduce the heat and poach until they are just set (about 2 minutes). Remove with a slotted spoon, peel and set aside. Return the shells, the boiling water and any juices to the stock. Add more water to cover.

Bring to the boil, stir well and simmer for 30 minutes. Strain through a fine sieve and reduce the liquid to 600 ml/1 pint. This makes a delicious stock.

Meanwhile, heat the remaining butter in a pan and fry the rice until it becomes opaque. Pour in the measured stock, add the saffron strands, season, cover and simmer gently until all the liquid has been absorbed. Cut up the prawns, remove the crab meat from the claws and add it to the rice, together with the Egg Sauce Base and grated Parmesan cheese.

Press the mixture into a buttered ring mould or 6 individual moulds, then turn out and serve, garnished with sprigs of watercress, diced tomato (warmed through) and snipped chives.

Serves 6

Crab Mousse

This isn't really a mousse; but it's not really a soufflé either. Anyway, it's delicious, easy and delicately light. It can be served in two ways, hot or cold - cook it quickly in a hot oven and it rises; cook it slowly with less heat and it is a delicate, savoury, cooked custard that can be eaten hot or cold.

To make a white sauce, melt the butter in a small pan, stir in the flour and cook for 1 minute. Pour in the milk and cook, whisking, until thickened. Pour into a liquidizer or food processor, add the crab meat, which will cool the mixture slightly (reserve a little white meat for garnish if serving the dish cold). Add the eggs, egg yolks and anchovy essence, if using, and purée until smooth.

Butter 6 ramekin dishes and divide the mixture between them. Place several sheets of newspaper in a roasting tin, place the ramekins on top and fill the tin with water to half way up the sides of the dishes.

To serve hot, cook the mousses while the mixture is still warm, in a preheated oven at 220°C (425°F) Gas Mark 7 for about 8 minutes until it rises into a soufflé. Season the Egg Sauce Base with salt and lemon juice, spoon over the mousse and serve immediately, garnished with sprigs of chervil. If the mixture is cold when you put it in the oven, it will take up to 20 minutes to cook.

To serve cold as a savoury custard, pour the mixture into the ramekins or individual tart tins, and cook in a preheated oven at 150°C (300°F) Gas Mark 2 for 25 minutes. Remove from the oven, cool, then turn them out on to starter plates.

To make the sauce, spoon 300 ml/½ pint Egg Sauce Base into a bowl or pan, thin out with water and lemon juice. Pour it around the crab custard, garnish with sprigs of chervil and white crab meat, and serve.
Serves 6

40 g/1½ oz butter

25 g/1 oz flour

300 ml/½ pint milk

1 small cooked crab or
250 g/8 oz mixed crab meat
(white and brown, but
mostly brown)

2 whole eggs and 2 egg yolks

1 teaspoon anchovy
essence, to taste (optional)

600 ml/1 pint Egg Sauce Base if
serving hot, or 300 ml/½ pint
if serving cold

lemon juice, to taste

sprigs of chervil, to garnish

salt and freshly
ground black pepper

King Prawns with Basil and Tomato Sauce

This produces a most beautiful, scented, light butter sauce – and is basically very simple. It takes only a few minutes to cook the prawns – do it yourself, because they must not be allowed to harden during cooking. The pre-cooked varieties I have tried are not suitable, but if you can find a fishmonger who cooks his shellfish properly, then, by all means, warm them and serve with the sauce, omitting the cooking liquid.

Roll out the pastry, cut into crescent shapes and mark into stripes with a fork. Glaze with milk or egg wash and cook in a preheated oven at 220°C (425°F) Gas Mark 7 for about 15 minutes, or until risen and golden. If time permits, turn off the oven, open it, and dry off the crescents until crisp right through.

To make the sauce flavouring, place the shallots, butter, vinegar and peppercorns in a stainless steel pan and simmer until syrupy. Pour in the water and boil furiously. Strain through a fine sieve into a pan, squeezing the shallots against the mesh to press out the flavour. Bring to the boil and reduce to 1 tablespoon.

Cut the tomatoes into tiny, neat cubes. Spread out on an ovenproof tray and sprinkle with salt. Set aside to heat under the grill later.

Slice the basil leaves into fine ribbons. Pour the Egg Sauce Base into a pan, heat gently and, using a balloon whisk, beat in the shredded basil leaves and flavouring. Season with salt and freshly ground black pepper and keep warm.

Place the uncooked prawns in cold water and heat to just below boiling point for about 2 minutes (just long enough to stiffen them). Lift them out, put aside and keep warm. Peel the prawns, but keep the tail fins intact. Remove and discard the black line running down the back of the prawns. Warm the tomatoes under the grill or in the oven.

Arrange the prawns on heated starter plates. Fold the heated cubes of tomato into the sauce without breaking them, then spoon the sauce over and around the prawns. Add the pastry crescents and garnish with sprigs of basil.

Serves 6

125 g/6 oz puff pastry

milk or egg wash for glaze

2 shallots, chopped

50 g/2 oz butter

150 ml/¼ pint white wine vinegar

10 whole black peppercorns

175 ml/6 fl oz water

3 Italian tomatoes, skinned and deseeded

about 10 sprigs of basil, plus extra, to garnish

300 ml/½ pint Egg Sauce Base

18 raw king prawns

salt and freshly ground black pepper

Steak Béarnaise

6 tender steaks, about
175-250 g/6-8 oz each

For the Béarnaise sauce:
50 g/2 oz butter

3 shallots, chopped

10 whole black
peppercorns, crushed

300 ml/½ pint tarragon vinegar

1 tablespoon chopped fresh
tarragon, plus 1 tablespoon extra

1 teaspoon dried tarragon

250 g/8 oz unsalted
butter (to be clarified)

300 ml/½ pint Egg Sauce Base

1 egg yolk

salt and freshly
ground black pepper

This – possibly the most delicious of all the steak sauces – is made quite separately from the meat. It is a thick chunky member of the sabayon family, but requires a higher proportion of clarified butter, plus an extra egg yolk to give it added density.

The shallot, which contributes a little sweetness to the sauce, is indispensable for absorbing the reducing vinegar. The final addition of chopped fresh tarragon gives extra flavour, but you may prefer your sauce smooth and creamy rather than speckled with green, in which case you should add it to the tarragon reduction, which will be strained out later.

To make the Béarnaise Sauce, place the butter, shallots, peppercorns, vinegar and fresh and dried tarragon into a non-metal or stainless steel pan and simmer until syrupy.

Add about 175 ml/6 fl oz water and boil furiously for a few minutes to draw the reduced vinegar flavouring from the shallots. Strain through a fine sieve, squeezing the shallots against the side, to extract all the flavour but leave the fibres and solids behind. Bring to the boil and reduce to 2 tablespoons. Set aside.

Heat the butter until it froths, allow to stand for 5 minutes, then skim off the froth. Pour the separated butter into another pan, and discard the buttermilk underneath. The butter is now clarified.

Make the Egg Sauce Base in a liquidizer, as described on page 14, add the egg yolks, the clarified butter and the 2 tablespoons of the concentrated liquid, extra fresh tarragon, and salt and pepper to taste. Blend until smooth.

Grill the steaks to taste and serve with the sauce – which could be served in an artichoke base for added panache.

Serves 6

Lamb in Pastry Paloise

Our most popular meat dish at the Horn of Plenty relies on the sauce for its delicious effect. A loin of lamb should feed four or five people, baked whole in pastry or cut into pieces and cooked separately. Remove any gristle from the meat before you roll it up in the pastry otherwise it will curl and burst through.

To make the duxelles (mushroom stuffing), heat the butter in a pan and cook the chopped onion until softened but not coloured. Add the mushrooms and cook until the juices evaporate and the mixture is dry. Otherwise it will steam as it cooks and make the pastry soggy.

Season with salt, the lemon zest and plenty of grated nutmeg and set aside in a sieve to drain and cool.

Remove the eye of the loin of lamb and the fillet from underneath the rib cage. Remove the gristly meat at the neck. Working from the tail end, remove the layer of gristle with a sharp knife, sliding and wiggling the knife up to the neck in the same way you skin a fillet of fish. The undercut should also be degristled in the same way.

Roll out the pastry to a rectangle a little longer than the meat and three times as wide. Season the meat and place it, without stretching, on the front edge of the pastry, with the fillet added to the neck end to even out the thickness. Place sprigs of fresh lemon thyme along the meat, cover with the mushroom mixture and roll the meat up tightly in the pastry, sealing and glazing it with egg wash. Set aside to rest.

To make the Paloise Sauce, place the vinegar, butter and chopped mint leaves in a pan, boil and reduce until most of the vinegary kick has evaporated (take care not to singe the vinegar). Add to the Egg Sauce Base, season and keep warm.

Cook in a preheated oven at 230°C (450°F) Gas Mark 8 for a total of about 20 minutes for pink, or 30 minutes well done.

To serve, cut off the hollow ends of the pastry first. Slice the meat and pastry to give 3 slices per person. Place on heated plates, spoon some of the sauce beside the meat and serve the remainder separately in a sauceboat. Steamed new potatoes and seasonal vegetables such as mangetout or sugar snap peas would be suitable accompaniments.

Serves 4–5

---

1 large loin of lamb
about 2.5 kg/5 lb

375 g/12 oz shortcrust
or puff pastry

sprigs of fresh lemon thyme

egg wash

salt and freshly
ground black pepper

For the duxelles:
50 g/2 oz unsalted butter

50 g/2 oz finely
chopped onion

125 g/4 oz finely
chopped mushrooms

grated zest of 1 lemon

¼ teaspoon grated nutmeg

For the paloise sauce:
150 ml/¼ pint
white wine vinegar

50 g/2 oz butter

1 bunch fresh mint,
finely chopped

250 ml/8 fl oz Egg Sauce Base

salt

Packets of Lamb with a Béarnaise Sauce

12 lamb cutlets

25 g/1 oz butter

50 g/2 oz onions, sliced

150 g/5 oz mushrooms, finely sliced

50 ml/2 fl oz brandy

50 ml/2 fl oz double cream

¼ teaspoon nutmeg

six 23 cm/9 inches rounds of flaky pastry

6 small slices of ham

egg wash

salt and freshly ground black pepper

For the Béarnaise sauce:
50 g/2 oz butter

3 shallots, chopped

10 whole black peppercorns, crushed

300 ml/½ pint tarragon vinegar

1 tablespoon chopped fresh tarragon

1 teaspoon dried tarragon

300 ml/½ pint Egg Sauce Base

250 g/8 oz unsalted butter (to be clarified)

1 tablespoon chopped fresh tarragon (optional)

A more robust and very different dish from the recipe for Lamb in Pastry Paloise on the previous page.

Make the Béarnaise Sauce according to the recipe for Steak Béarnaise on page 40, adding 2 teaspoons of tomato purée at the end.

To prepare the lamb, first remove the bones from the cutlets and trim them neatly, discarding excess fat. Remove the resulting flap, or wrap it around the eye of the cutlet and skewer it in place.

Heat the butter in a large pan, add the cutlets and brown at a high heat, for about 10 seconds on each side, turning once. Season with salt and freshly ground black pepper, then remove the meat and set aside to cool. Remove the skewers when cold.

Add the onions to the pan, cook until just beginning to brown, then add the mushrooms and cook them through. Finally add the brandy and cook gently until the alcohol has boiled off. Pour in the cream and boil until thickened. Season with nutmeg, salt and freshly ground black pepper and leave to cool.

Spread out the pastry rounds on a flat surface and place two cutlets on each, one on top of the other, with a spoonful of the mushroom mixture in between. Cover with a slice of ham.

Gather up the edges of each completed pastry round and squeeze into a sack shape. Cut out the excess pastry and brush the parcels with the egg yolk wash.

Cook in a preheated oven at 230°C (450°F) Gas Mark 8 for about 20 minutes or until the pastry is brown. Serve with the Béarnaise Sauce. Lyonnaise potatoes, braised chicory or braised fennel are all suitable accompaniments.

Serves 6

Braised Leg of Lamb with Caper Sauce

It seems a shame that, just because mutton has virtually disappeared from butchers' shops, the traditional accompaniment of capers in white sauce has also gone. The flavour of lamb is gentler but the sauce can still be used to great effect, though it should be less piquant than it would have been with mutton.

Place the garlic, onions, rosemary, peppercorns, bay leaf, chopped thyme, parsley, bacon rinds or bacon, a little salt with the measured water in a large saucepan and boil for 5 minutes.

Place the leg of lamb in a large roasting tin. Whisk the *beurre-manié* into the mixture in the saucepan, then pour it all over the lamb in the roasting tin. Cover with aluminium foil and seal well.

Cook in a preheated oven at 160°C (325°F) Gas Mark 3 for about 30 minutes. Uncover the lamb, turn it over, re-seal and return it to the oven. Repeat this procedure every 20 minutes for the next 1½ hours.

Remove the lamb and pierce with a skewer. If the juices run clear, remove and set aside in a warm place. If not, return it to the oven and cook a little longer.

Strain off the cooking liquid into a jug and cover the meat to keep warm. When the fat has risen to the surface, spoon it off and pour the liquid underneath into a small saucepan. Bring to the boil and reduce to about 600 ml/1 pint.

Drain the capers, squeeze dry and chop finely. Place the Egg Sauce Base in a liquidizer or food processor, add the capers and the lamb cooking liquid and purée briefly to blend the flavours. Taste and adjust the seasoning. To serve, carve the meat in the usual way, and serve the sauce from a bowl with a ladle. Mashed potatoes, with boiled carrots or broad beans would be suitable accompaniments.

Serves 6

1 clove garlic, sliced

3 onions, sliced,

1 sprig of rosemary

12 whole black peppercorns

1 bay leaf

1 tablespoon chopped fresh thyme leaves, or 1 teaspoon dried

1 tablespoon chopped fresh flat leaf parsley

a few bacon rinds or rashers of streaky bacon

1.8 litres/3 pints water

1 whole leg of lamb, about 3 kg/6 lb

beurre manié, made with 50 g/2 oz flour mixed with 70 g/2½ oz butter

For the caper sauce: 325 g/11 oz bottled capers, drained

300 ml/½ pint Egg Sauce Base

salt and freshly ground black pepper

Pot-au-feu of Poached Gammon Hock

2 or 3 gammon hocks,
smoked or green

6 medium small onions

3 carrots

3 cloves

1 bay leaf

12 small potatoes

1 large leek, white
part only, chopped

3 small kohlrabi, quartered

1 medium Savoy cabbage,
sliced into 6 wedges

300 ml/½ pint Egg Sauce Base

salt and freshly
ground black pepper

There is a good deal of meat on the hock and it is delicious simmered with root vegetables, with the cabbage and Egg Sauce Base added later. Serve with some delicate green vegetables prepared separately to enhance it yet further.

Poule au Pot (recipe below left) is a traditional French peasant dish and wonderful prepared this way. Henry IV of France – estimable man – vowed that every Frenchman should have a Poule au Pot on the table every Sunday (but only if God granted him a long life!)

Kohlrabi is a handsome vegetable, which deserves to be used much more often. Interestingly, it is particularly delicious eaten raw! It is even better when you grow it yourself, and can use it before the skin becomes hard.

If the hocks are salty, bring them to the boil in fresh water and then discard the water. Then start all over again!

Put the onions, carrots, cloves and bay leaf into a deep pot, and place the hocks on top. Cover with cold water, bring to the boil and simmer for 2 hours.

Add the potatoes, chopped leek and kohlrabi, and simmer for about 10 minutes. Add the cabbage and continue simmering for a further 20 minutes, until everything is tender and cooked through.

Strain off the liquid into a saucepan, bring to the boil and reduce to about 900 ml/1½ pints, the extent of the reduction depending on the flavour. Beat about 1 ladleful into the Egg Sauce Base, then beat in the remainder. Taste and adjust the seasoning.

Carefully remove the hocks from the pot, discard the skin and bone and return the pieces of meat to the pot. Serve on heated dinner plates with the sauce spooned over and around.

Serves 6

Alternatively:
POULE AU POT
Instead of the gammon, substitute a boiling fowl if you can find one, or a large roasting chicken. Serve with Herb Dumplings (page 150) or with the lemon stuffing on page 49, tied in muslin and poached for the last 30 minutes of cooking time.

Rabbit in White Wine with a Gooseberry Sauce

50 g/2 oz butter

25 g/1 oz chopped, fresh flat leaf parsley

2 sprigs of thyme

1 bay leaf

3 large shallots, chopped

150 ml/¼ pint white wine, white port or white vermouth300 ml/½ pint chicken stock

125 g/4 oz fresh gooseberries

12 smoked bacon rashers

2 good sized rabbits, jointed

150 ml/¼ pint Egg Sauce Base

1 tablespoon chopped fresh herbs, to garnish

salt and freshly ground black pepper

Rabbit has a gentle, rather bland, flavour and I find that, like fish, it blossoms when you add a little acidity. The three different kinds of alcohol give a slightly different flavour to the dish; white wine gives a dryer taste, white port is sweeter and white vermouth is rather seasoned. Gooseberry juice is used here as a souring agent instead of the verjuice (unripe grape juice) which was used years ago.

Heat the butter in a small pan, add the herbs and shallots and cook until softened but not coloured. Add the wine, bring to the boil and reduce until syrupy. Add the stock and gooseberries, bring to the boil and add seasoning.

Roll the bacon rashers round the rabbit pieces and tuck the parcels into a casserole or slow cooker. Cover with the hot stock, cover and simmer for about 1–1½ hours, or until the meat is tender. Carefully lift out the rabbit and place in a deep flat-based dish.

Bring the liquid in the pot to the boil and reduce until you have about 300 ml/½ pint of liquid with good flavour.

Strain into a clean pan, pushing through the gooseberry flesh which will help to thicken it. Add the Egg Sauce Base, taste and adjust the seasoning and consistency – it should be quite creamy. If too thick, add a little water to thin it out. Reheat but do not boil.

Pour over the rabbit and garnish with chopped fresh herbs. Creamy mashed potatoes or a purée of dried broad beans would be suitable accompaniments.

Serves 6

Alternatively:
RABBIT WITH MUSTARD AND GOOSEBERRY SAUCE

Mustard is a traditional accompaniment for rabbit. Add 2 tablespoon Dijon mustard at the same time as the Egg Sauce Base and proceed as in the main recipe.

Partridge or Spatchcocked Poussins on a Bed of Cabbage

If using partridge, heat the butter in a pan and brown the birds, skin-side down. Place the partridges in an oiled roasting tin and cook in a preheated oven at 200°C (400°F) Gas Mark 6 for 25–30 minutes, according to the age of the bird, until done.

Meanwhile, add the wine to the frying pan and reduce until syrupy. Add the stock, cabbage, bacon and caraway seeds, cover the pan and cook until softened. Uncover and fast-boil to drive off any liquid. When the birds are done, remove and keep warm, then reduce the juices and add to the cabbage mixture. Remove from the heat, stir in the Egg Sauce Base, and serve with on heated dinner plates with the roasted birds on top.

If using spatchcocked poussins, rub them with oil and the chopped herbs, season and grill the underside first, then turn over and grill, skin-side up, for 20–25 minutes. Melt the butter in a small pan, add the wine and proceed as before.

Serves 6

6 grey-legged partridges, or spatchcocked poussins

50 g/2 oz butter

olive oil, for brushing

150 ml/¼ pint white wine

150 ml/¼ pint chicken stock

1 small white cabbage, shredded

125 g/4 oz bacon, sliced

1 tablespoon caraway seeds

150 ml/¼ pint Egg Sauce Base

6 tablespoons chopped mixed thyme, parsley and marjoram

salt and pepper

Chicken and Fennel Sauce

Quarter the fennel and chop the tops and outer leaves. Heat half the butter in a large pan and lightly fry the chicken pieces all over until lightly browned. Remove from the pan.

Heat the remaining butter, add the fennel quarters and cook until softened but not coloured. Add the garlic and cook until the fennel and garlic have become lightly coloured.

Add the wine and Pernod, and reduce until syrupy. Add the stock, the chicken and seasoning. Cover and simmer for about 30 minutes, until cooked. Remove the chicken and fennel, and keep warm.

Add the chopped fennel, bring to the boil and reduce to about 150 ml/¼ pint. Off the heat, whisk in the Egg Sauce Base. Place the chicken and fennel on heated dinner plates and pour the sauce over.

Serves 6

3 fennel bulbs

125 g/4 oz butter

1.5 kg/3 lb chicken, jointed

2 cloves garlic, crushed

150 ml/¼ pint white wine

1 teaspoon Pernod

600 ml/1 pint chicken stock

300 ml/½ pint Egg Sauce Base

salt and pepper

Turkey Breasts stuffed with Fresh Summer Herbs

A delightful summery change from the usual chestnut, sage or rice stuffings usually associated with turkey at Christmas.

This stuffing and cooking method is delicious in the variation for this recipe, Poached Trout stuffed with Fresh Summer Herbs. Gut and bone the trout along its backbone, leaving the belly skin intact. Set the fish on their bellies in a shallow, ovenproof dish, open out the cavity on top and fill with the stuffing. Cover the dish with foil and place in the oven for about 15 minutes.

Make a slit in one end of each turkey breast to create a large bag. Season it inside with salt and freshly ground black pepper.

To make the stuffing, place the egg, lemon zest and juice, parsley, thyme and tarragon in a liquidizer or food processor and blend until smooth. Spoon into a bowl and add one-third of the Egg Sauce Base, together with the breadcrumbs to mop up the liquid. Season to taste and add the pistachio nuts. Place inside the turkey breasts.

Wrap the breasts in clingfilm, making large sausage shapes, then wrap them again in foil. Place in an ovenproof casserole, pour in about 300 ml/½ pint of boiling water, cover and cook in a preheated oven at 120°C (250°F) Gas Mark ½ for 40 minutes.

Remove the turkey breasts, unwrap them carefully, and keep warm. Pour the chicken stock into a pan, add the juices which have come out of the wrappings, bring to the boil and reduce to about 300 ml/½ pint. Beat in the remaining Egg Sauce Base and the chopped chervil. Taste and adjust the seasoning.

Slice each turkey breast crossways and place on heated dinner plates. Pour over the sauce, and garnish with sprigs of chervil, parsley, lemon thyme and tarragon and sprinkle over chopped pistachio nuts and lemon zest. Serve with new potatoes, such as pink fir apples, and steamed sugar snap peas or flat beans.

Serves 6

2 small turkey breasts

1 egg

zest and juice of 1 lemon

large bunch of parsley

leaves of 3 sprigs of fresh lemon thyme

1 tablespoon chopped fresh tarragon

150 ml/¼ pint Egg Sauce Base

50 g/2 oz fresh breadcrumbs

25 g/1 oz chopped pistachio nuts

300 ml/½ pint chicken stock

2 tablespoons chopped fresh chervil

salt and freshly ground black pepper

To garnish:
sprigs of chervil, parsley, lemon thyme and tarragon

chopped pistachio nuts

lemon zest

Alternatively:
POACHED TROUT
Substitute 6 trout, boned as described above left, instead of the turkey breasts, and proceed as in the main recipe, cooking for about 15 minutes.

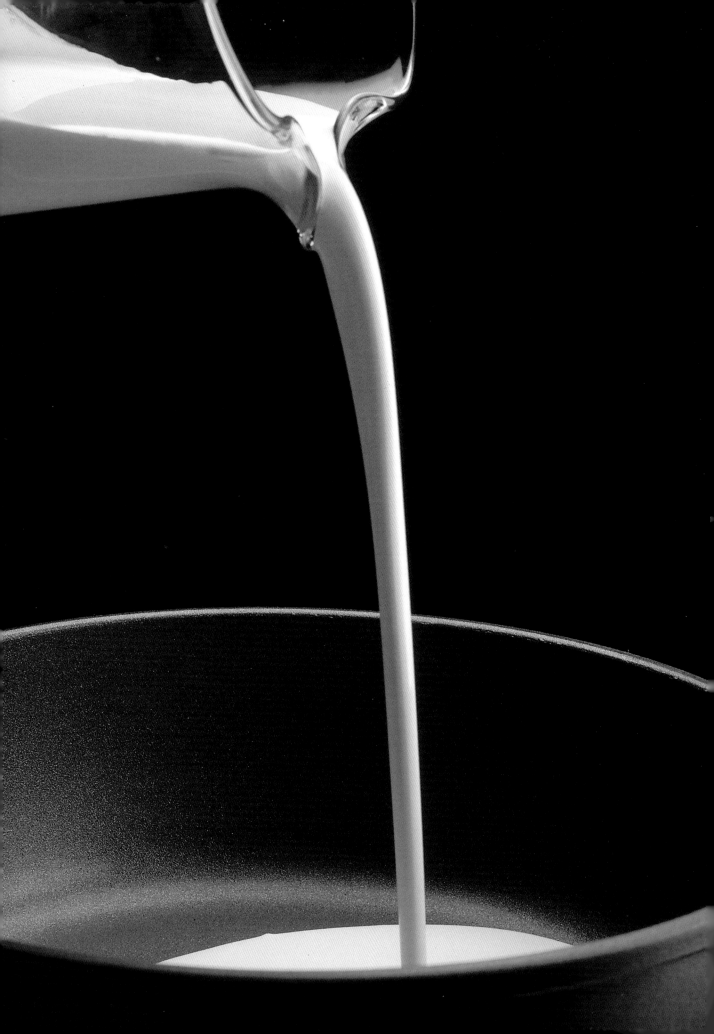

cream
SAUCE BASE

QUICK AND SIMPLE, Cream Sauces can be adapted to many different uses and dishes – as a first course with seafood or vegetables; with meat, chicken or game as a main course; and of course where you would most expect to find it – used in ice-creams and puddings.

If you understand just how a Cream Sauce Base works, it will make it much easier to manipulate when you adapt it to this great variety of dishes.

Basically cream is a balance of milk solids, water and fat and, provided it has been pasteurized, there is no danger of normal fresh cream curdling when you bring it to the boil.

Use whipping cream rather than double cream, since it doesn't have such a blanketing effect on the final flavour. In fact, all the recipes in this book should be made with whipping cream unless otherwise stated – the exceptions are those few recipes made with lovely, lemony crème fraîche.

When you boil cream, you will find it thickens very quickly, and the size of the bubbles is a very good indication of thickness in cream, or indeed any boiling liquid. The larger the bubbles, the thicker the sauce or liquid.

And – a final hint which I cannot stress too often. If you want to thin out the Cream Sauce Base, use water – not more cream.

1 Bring the cream to the boil in a non-stick pan until it bubbles fiercely with small bubbles, and forms a POURING CONSISTENCY.

2 The Cream Sauce Base continues to reduce, boiling with large bubbles and forming a much thicker, COATING CONSISTENCY.

3 The Cream Sauce Base has now thickened into a thick, mayonnaise-like EMULSION, and has become richer and darker in colour.

A Cream Sauce Base is made in three stages, and it can be used in recipes at any one of these stages, as outlined below. Stages 4 and 5 show it 'going too far', but even at Stage 6, it can be used as a 'Beurre Noisette' sauce.

1 Pour the cream into a non-stick pan and bring to the boil. Cook until it bubbles fiercely with small bubbles and thickens to a POURING CONSISTENCY. Use in this form for recipes such as Leek Mousse with Chervil or Tarragon Sauce (page 54), Red Bream with a Sauce of Three Zests (page 68) or Roast Saddle of Hare in a Creamy Sauce (page 91).
2 Continue to boil the cream, stirring, until it reduces and thickens further and boils with big bubbles to form a COATING CONSISTENCY. Use it in this form for recipes such as Broad Beans with Ham and Cream (page 57), Chicken in Creamed Curry Sauce (page 80), or Mussels with Saffron (page 75).

Braised Chicory with Ham and Cheese

A generous starter, or a satisfying luncheon dish when served with a salad. Don't add salt because the ham contains enough.

Roll the ham slices round the heads of chicory and lay them close together in a small ovenproof dish. Pour around the stock or water, sprinkle with the herbs and cover the dish with foil.

Cook in a preheated oven at 150°C (300°F) Gas Mark 2 for 30–40 minutes. Remove from the oven, drain off the stock or water, place the cheese slices over the ham and chicory and put aside to keep warm.

Pour the cream into a non-stick pan, add any pan juices, bring to the boil and reduce until slightly thickened as in Step 1, page 52. Remove from the heat and beat in the egg yolk. Add the chopped chives and pour over the cheese and chicory. Sieve the breadcrumbs and sprinkle over the top, place under a hot grill until browned, then serve.

Serves 6

6 slices of ham, from the bone

6 heads of chicory

1 tablespoon chopped, mixed fresh thyme and parsley

6 slices Gruyère cheese

Cream Sauce Base, made from 300 ml/½ pint whipping cream

1 egg yolk, beaten

1 tablespoon chopped fresh chives

50 g/2 oz dry white breadcrumbs

freshly ground black pepper

Creamed Jerusalem Artichokes

Artichokes are a nuisance to peel, but this method will ensure their flavour isn't lost in the cooking water.

Rinse the artichokes thoroughly, but do not peel them. Add them to a large pan of boiling, salted water. Return to the boil, reduce the heat, and simmer until tender. Drain and, when cool enough to handle, slit the skin and peel it off. If the small knobs break off, remove the flesh from the insides with a teaspoon.

Pour the cream into a non-stick pan, add the herbs and plenty of pepper, bring to the boil and reduce to a mayonnaise-like emulsion, as in Step 3, page 52. Season to taste and fold in the artichoke pieces.

Thin with a little water if necessary, but don't boil again.

Serves 6

1.5 kg/3 lb unpeeled Jerusalem artichokes

Cream Sauce Base, made from 300 ml/½ pint whipping cream

1 tablespoon chopped fresh chervil or flat leaf parsley

salt and freshly ground black pepper

Salad of Fruits with Sweet-sour Cream

Cream Sauce Base, made from 150 ml/¼ pint whipping cream

2 tablespoons Dijon mustard

1 tablespoon white wine vinegar

1 tablespoon sugar

2.5 cm/1 inch piece of preserved stem ginger

300 ml/½ pint sunflower oil

3 small firm melons; green Galia, orange Charentais or Canteloupe

250 g/8 oz seedless grapes, halved

3 kiwifruit, peeled and sliced

Use this sweet-sour cream dressing on any salad, thinning it out with water if necessary. The salad also works well with a little chopped Parma ham added.

To make the Cream Sauce Base, pour the cream into a non-stick pan and boil until to a coating consistency, as in Step 2, page 52.

Transfer to a liquidizer, then add the mustard, vinegar, sugar and ginger. Blend briefly, then add the oil, a little at a time, as if you were making mayonnaise. Pour into a bowl, adding a little water if the emulsion is not smooth enough.

Cut the melons in half and remove the seeds. Slice a piece from the base so each half will stand flat on a plate. Place the grapes and kiwifruit in a small bowl, stir in the dressing to coat, then spoon into the melon centres and serve.

Alternatively, peel and slice the melon and kiwifruit, arrange on a salad plate with the grapes, then spoon over the dressing.

Serves 6

Garlic Potato Salad with Ham and Celery

500 g/1 lb new potatoes

250 g/8 oz good sliced ham

3 young celery sticks, sliced

1 clove garlic, crushed

Cream Sauce Base, made from 300 ml/½ pint whipping cream

1 tablespoon lemon juice

salt and freshly ground black pepper

Another way of making a salad dressing, using the Cream Sauce Base rather than mayonnaise to bind the potatoes.

Cook the potatoes, cut them into chunks and the ham into strips. Mix the ham, potatoes, celery and garlic gently in a large bowl.

Pour the cream into a non-stick pan, bring to the boil, reduce to a pouring consistency, as in Step 1, page 52. Cool, add seasoning and lemon juice, then spoon over the salad. Fold in quickly, stopping the moment the mixture loses its creaminess. This will happen more quickly than usual, because of the lemon juice. Taste and adjust the seasoning and serve.

Serves 6

Potato Gratin with Pickled Herrings

Herring adds an unusual flavour to this delicious potato gratin. Available early in the season, waxy potato varieties include Maris Bard, Pentland Javelin, Rocket, or the yellow ones simply labelled as 'Mediterranean potatoes'.

If using rollmops, unwrap the herrings and discard the pickled onion and the toothpick. Slice the fish into 2.5 cm/1 inch pieces.

To make the Cream Sauce Base, pour the cream into a non-stick pan, bring to the boil and reduce to a pouring consistency, as in Step 1, page 52. Taste and adjust the seasoning, then add the potato slices, one at a time, so they don't stick to each other.

Butter a large, flat, ovenproof dish, add a layer of potato, then a layer of onion and two fillets of herring. Repeat twice more, finishing with a layer of potato. Pour over any remaining cream and sprinkle with breadcrumbs.

Cook in a preheated oven at 160°C (325°F) Gas Mark 3 for about 10–20 minutes. Brown under the grill if necessary.

Serves 6

6 pickled herring fillets (e.g. rollmops or Bismarck)

Cream Sauce Base, made from 600 ml/1 pint whipping cream

750 g/1½ lb waxy potatoes, sliced and cooked

2 medium onions, sliced

fine toasted breadcrumbs

salt and freshly ground black pepper

Broad Beans with Ham and Cream

The outer skins of broad beans are tough and coarse late in the year. Remove them and the taste is transformed – well worth the trouble.

Simmer the beans until the centres are tender but not powdery. Drain and refresh under cold running water until cool enough to handle. Remove the outer, greyish skin and discard.

To make the Cream Sauce Base, pour the cream into a non-stick pan, bring to the boil and reduce to a pouring consistency, as in Step 1, page 52. Add the ham, beans and parsley. Reheat, taste and adjust the seasoning, and serve when nicely coated with the cream.

Serves 6

3 kg/6 lb broad beans (not young ones, nor floury old ones)

Cream Sauce Base, made from 75 ml/3 fl oz double cream

125 g/4 oz English ham, chopped (or 50 g/2 oz prosciutto)

1 tablespoon chopped, fresh, flat leaf parsley

salt and freshly ground black pepper

Salmon Quenelles in a Creamy Wine Sauce

500 g/1 lb salmon tail, about 275 g/9 oz filleted

6 egg whites

375 ml/13 fl oz double cream

salt

For the creamy wine sauce:
75 ml/3 fl oz white wine

75 ml/3 fl oz white vermouth

50 g/2 oz butter

300 ml/½ pint fish stock

1 tablespoon white roux (see below)

Cream Sauce Base, made from 300 ml/½ pint whipping cream

salt and freshly ground black pepper

To garnish:
sprigs of chervil

salmon caviar (optional

Note:

WHITE ROUX
A roux is used to thicken sauces. Melt some butter in a heavy-based saucepan, add a little less than an equal quantity of flour and cook for a few minutes, stirring, until the mixture is frothy and the flour is cooked.

I was lucky enough to be invited into the kitchen of La Mère Brazier, a French three-star Michelin chef famous for her quenelles, to learn her method of making them – different from mine. Her way was wonderful but very difficult, so I continued to make them this way. It serves eight as a starter or six as a main course for lunch.

To make the sauce, pour the wine and vermouth into a pan, add half the butter, bring to the boil again and reduce until syrupy. Add the fish stock, return to the boil and reduce to 250 ml/8 fl oz, with a good flavour (which depends on the quality of your stock).

Whisk in the cream, bring to the boil and simmer until it reaches a coating consistency, as in Step 2, page 52. Season with salt and plenty of pepper and whisk in the remaining butter.

To make the quenelles, place the salmon, egg whites and salt into a liquidizer or food processor and purée until smooth. Add the cream, whisking until the mixture stiffens, check the salt, then chill.

(It is easier to add the cream to the liquidizer, but be very careful or it may turn to butter – a disaster that cannot be rectified. So, if in doubt, turn it into a bowl and whisk it with an electric whisk or by hand. To remove any filaments, force the mixture through a sieve into a bowl before placing in the refrigerator. This is optional but makes a finer mixture and therefore a more delicate quenelle.)

To cook the quenelles, bring a large pan of salted water to the boil. Turn it to just simmering, dip a dessertspoon into the simmering water and then take up a dollop of the quenelle mixture, and roll it against the side of the bowl to produce an egg-shaped quenelle. Again dip the loaded spoon into the simmering water, turn it over and tap the quenelle off into the water. Repeat the procedure for each quenelle. Poach each one for 8 minutes, then remove with a slotted spoon, set aside and keep warm. Do not let the water boil or they will break up, and don't cover the pan or the quenelles will soufflé.

To serve, place 2–3 quenelles on each heated plate, pour over the sauce and serve immediately, garnished with sprigs of chervil and a spoonful of salmon caviar (optional).

Serves 6

Dover Sole in a White Wine Sauce with Mushrooms

Cream Sauce Base made from
300 ml/½ pint whipping cream

200 g/7 oz unsalted butter

2 shallots, chopped

300 ml/½ pint white vermouth

150 ml/½ pint fish stock

6 Dover soles, about
500 g/1 lb each, skinned on
both sides

125 g/4 oz
button mushrooms

½ teaspoon lemon juice

1 egg yolk, to glaze

salt and freshly
ground black pepper

For the finest texture, taste and appearance, you should always cook sole on the bone. Then, as soon as the fish is cool enough to handle, remove the fillets with a fish slice and serve immediately or roll them flat in foil and gently reheat when needed.

To make the Cream Sauce Base, pour the whipping cream into a pan, bring to the boil and reduce by half to a coating consistency, as in Step 2, page 52. Set aside.

Heat 50 g/2 oz of the butter in a saucepan, add the shallots and the vermouth and simmer until syrupy. Add the fish stock and a very little salt, bring to the boil, then pour into a roasting tin.

Place the fishes in the stock and cover the tin with foil. Cook in a preheated oven at 140°C (275°F) Gas Mark 1, for about 10 minutes or until the fillets will just pull away along the backbone.

Using a fish slice, carefully remove all 4 fillets from each fish. If you wish to use them immediately, place them in a heated serving dish and keep warm. Otherwise, roll them lengthways in foil until you are ready to reheat.

Heat 75 g/2 oz of the butter in a small pan and sauté the button mushrooms until soft. Sprinkle with a little lemon juice and salt, then scatter them over the fish.

To make the sauce, strain the fish-poaching stock into a saucepan, pressing all the juices through, and reduce to 150 ml/¼ pint. Whisk in the Cream Sauce Base, any juices which have come out of the fish, and the remaining butter.

Whisk the egg yolk with 2 teaspoons water over a gentle heat until frothy (but do not scramble). Add the froth to the sauce, then pour over the fish. Glaze under a hot grill until brown.

Serves 6

Parcels of Lemon Sole stuffed with Mushrooms and Scallops

There is a world of difference between a Dover sole and a lemon sole. Lemon sole is a type of plaice which, therefore, needs to be super-fresh to show off its flavour. Use spinach or young cabbage instead of Swiss chard leaves if you like, though chard is easier to handle.

Blanch the chard leaves by placing in a large pan of boiling water. Remove and refresh in cold water as soon as they are supple.

To make the Cream Sauce Base, place the cream in a non-stick pan, bring to the boil and reduce to a coating consistency, as in Step 2, page 52.

Heat half the butter in a frying pan, add the mushrooms, shallots and grated lemon zest and simmer until cooked dry. Season with salt and nutmeg, then cool. Spoon into a liquidizer or food processor, add the white part of the scallops (omitting the corals) and the egg yolks and purée until smooth. Turn out and stir in the double cream (but without overbeating). Taste and adjust the seasoning.

Spread the mixture over each fillet of sole and roll it up loosely.

Line 6 ramekin dishes with foil, then line with the chard leaves, with the most attractive part of the leaf on the bottom. Add the rolled fillets, spooning in a bit more stuffing mixture around the edges. Fold over the chard leaves and enclose in the foil. Firm down into a sound package, turn out of the ramekins and steam above boiling water for 15 minutes until firm. Set aside and keep warm.

To prepare the sauce, pour the vermouth into a pan, add the rest of the butter, bring to the boil and reduce to a syrup. Add the fish stock and Cream Sauce Base and bring to the boil. If you have any, prick the scallop roes and poach them in the sauce for a few seconds until very firm, then cut them into chunks and return to the sauce. Add the mango cubes, if using, and warm through.

Unwrap the foil and place each chard-wrapped parcel in the centre of a heated dinner plate. Pour the sauce round the parcels, brushing the chard leaves with a little melted butter to make them shine.

Serves 6

12 large leaves of Swiss chard

Cream Sauce Base, made from 600 ml/1 pint whipping cream

50 g/2 oz butter

125 g/4 oz mushrooms, roughly chopped

3 shallots, finely chopped

grated zest of 1 lemon

½ teaspoon nutmeg

6 scallops, cleaned

3 egg yolks

75 ml/3 fl oz double cream

6 fillets of lemon sole

275 ml/9 fl oz white vermouth

275 ml/9 fl oz concentrated fish stock

1 large, ripe mango, peeled, stoned and cut into cubes (optional)

melted butter, for brushing

salt and freshly ground black pepper

Skate Wings in a Nut-brown Sauce with Capers

When you buy skate, the most important rule is that if it smells strongly of ammonia – don't!

This unpleasant smell doesn't necessarily mean that it isn't fresh, but the pungency will become rapidly worse with age (not better, as some books say). Some skate wings have the smell and some do not.

This fish is extra good when filleted – it allows the thin strands to shrink and firm up, whereas when left on the bone they are stretched and easily overcook into a mush.

A good fishmonger will do this for you, but if not, it is very easy to do yourself. Run the tip of your knife down the long edge of the triangle, then gently work the knife flat towards the outer edges. A bendy filleting knife is best.

Fillet the skate as described above, or have your fishmonger do it for you. Season with salt and freshly ground black pepper.

Heat the hazelnut oil in a small pan and gently fry the mushrooms. Set aside and keep warm.

Heat the butter in a large frying pan. Fry the skate wings, turning them once, until they have shrunk and tightened up (this will happen very quickly – in just a minute or so).

To make the Cream Sauce Base, pour the cream into a non-stick pan, bring to the boil and cook until it begins to fry and toast the milk solids. Do not let it burn. (This is the *Beurre Noisette* effect in Step 6, page 53.)

Add the vinegar and boil again until it has almost disappeared, then pour in the cooking butter from the skate. Add the capers and chopped parsley, some salt and plenty of pepper.

To serve, place the skate wings and sautéed mushrooms on heated dinner plates, pour over the sauce and sprinkle with chopped fresh flat leaf parsley.

Serves 6

skate wings, skinned, for 6 people

1 tablespoon hazelnut oil

150 g/5 oz wild mushrooms or yellow oyster mushrooms

75 g/3 oz butter

Cream Sauce Base, made from 300 ml/½ pint whipping cream

150 ml/¼ pint white wine vinegar or raspberry vinegar

50 g/2 oz capers

3 tablespoons chopped fresh flat leaf parsley, plus extra, to garnish

salt and freshly ground black pepper

Note:

BEURRE NOISETTE

Beurre Noisette – Nut-brown Sauce – is usually made with butter. When made with cream (see Step 6, page 53) it has an even more delicious, nutty flavour and texture.

It is also easier to make than with butter – because it doesn't burn so fast. Make double the quantity and freeze the leftovers to flavour many other dishes, such as Sea Bass with Mustard Sauce on page 28.

Poached Trout with Green Herb Sauce

6 small trout, cleaned and gutted, with the heads left on

For the sauce:
175 g/6 oz butter

2 celery sticks, chopped

1 onion, chopped

250 ml/8 fl oz white vermouth

75 g/3 oz watercress

25 g/1 oz sorrel

6 sage leaves

6 large sprigs of chervil

12 mint leaves

125 g/4 oz cooked leeks

50 g/2 oz cooked spinach

Cream Sauce Base, made from 300 ml/½ pint whipping cream

grated zest of 1 lemon

grated nutmeg

salt and freshly ground black pepper

Alternatively:
HERBY CHICKEN
Prepare 6 skinless, boneless chicken breasts as described in the introduction. Proceed as in the main recipe.

This is a wonderful trout recipe – poaching is one of the healthiest ways to prepare any fish, as well as being one of the most delicious.

The recipe is particularly good for a dinner party – the green part of the sauce can be made in advance, leaving only the creamy bits to complete it.

If you are adapting the sauce to use with chicken, thicken the cream a little more than for trout, to allow for the cooking juices to be added at the end. The chicken breasts should be seasoned with salt, pepper, lemon zest and nutmeg, dotted with butter, wrapped in foil and steamed for 20–25 minutes.

Melt half the butter in a small pan, add 25 ml/1 fl oz water, the celery and onion, and cook until softened but not coloured. Add the white vermouth, bring to the boil and reduce to about 2 tablespoons.

Finely chop the watercress, sorrel, sage, chervil and mint, add to the vermouth mixture, and cook for 5 minutes, until most of the liquid has evaporated. Add the cooked leeks and spinach. Place in a liquidizer or food processor for a few seconds to chop and mix all the ingredients – but do not purée. Set aside.

Meanwhile, pour the cream into a pan, bring to the boil for a few minutes and reduce until slightly thickened, as in Step 1, page 52. Reheat the herb and vermouth mixture and add to the cream sauce. Season with salt, plenty of pepper, lemon zest and a little nutmeg.

To poach the trout, bring salted water to the boil in a large pan or fish kettle. Lower in the trout and immediately remove the pan from the heat. The fish will be done when the flesh inside the cavity near the backbone is no longer a raw pink in colour – about 8–10 minutes.

Lift out the trout, drain and pat dry with a cloth. Place the fish on heated dinner plates, and spoon the sauce at the side.
Serves 6

Baked Trout in Alsatian Riesling with Creamy Morels

Use any good Riesling in this dish, but since Riesling and morels are both typical ingredients in Alsace, I have used an Alsatian wine.

This delicious sauce can also be used with a poached chicken breast, served with rice, some tiny shrimp and sliced hard-boiled egg.

Place the dried morels in a small bowl, cover with boiling water and set aside to steep overnight.

Next day, drain the morels, retaining the soaking liquid. Rinse them free from sand and dirt. Strain the soaking liquid through muslin into a small saucepan. Bring to the boil, add the morels and simmer for a few minutes. Set aside.

To make the Cream Sauce Base, pour the cream into a pan, bring to the boil and reduce to a coating consistency, as in Step 2, page 52.

Heat the butter in a small pan and gently cook the garlic, bay leaf, cloves and onion until softened but not coloured. Add the wine, bring to the boil and reduce until syrupy. Add the fish stock.

Season the fish with salt, pepper and nutmeg, and place them in a baking dish or roasting pan. Pour over the flavoured liquid and cover the dish with foil. Cook the trout in a preheated oven at 180°C (350°F) Gas Mark 4 for about 20 minutes, or until the fish is done.

Carefully strain off the fish juices into a small pan. Add the morel cooking liquid, bring to the boil and reduce to a concentrate. Add the cooked morels and Cream Sauce Base, bring to the boil and simmer to amalgamate the flavours.

Remove from the heat and whisk in the egg yolks, if using, one at a time, then reheat (but do not boil). Taste and adjust the seasoning.

To serve, carefully remove the top skin from the trout, place the fish on heated dinner plates and pour the sauce around.

Serves 6

---

25 g/1 oz dried morels

Cream Sauce Base made from 300 ml/½ pint whipping cream

125 g/4 oz butter

1 clove garlic, chopped

1 bay leaf

4 cloves

1 onion, chopped

300 ml/½ pint Alsatian Riesling or other medium-dry white wine

285 ml/10 fl oz fish stock

6 small trout, cleaned and gutted, with heads left on

a pinch of nutmeg

2 egg yolks (optional)

salt and freshly ground black pepper

Alternatively:

POACHED ALSATIAN CHICKEN BREASTS

Lightly fry 6 chicken breasts in butter until pale golden on each side. Place in a baking dish and proceed as in the main recipe, substituting chicken stock for fish stock.

Red Mullet on Croûtes with Tomatoes and Mushrooms

Cream Sauce Base, made from
150 ml/¼ pint whipping cream

75 g/3 oz butter

125 ml/4 fl oz olive oil,
plus 3 tablespoons extra

1 onion, sliced

1 clove garlic, chopped

125 g/4 oz button
mushrooms, sliced

2 beefsteak tomatoes,
skinned, deseeded and chopped

½ teaspoon powdered bay leaf

1 teaspoon chopped fresh thyme
leaves or ½ teaspoon dried

275 ml/9 fl oz brandy

1 tablespoon shredded fresh basil
leaves, plus extra, for garnish

3 red mullet, about 500 g/1 lb
each, scaled and filleted
with livers reserved

6 rectangular slices
of buttered bread

75 ml/3 fl oz white vermouth

150 ml/¼ pint fish stock

salt and freshly
ground black pepper

Cornish red mullet, which I use, has a strong, almost spicy flavour, which is accentuated by using the large liver. The frozen imported variety, however, has comparatively little flavour and virtually no liver but it does have a firm flesh and good colour. The bones pull out of the fillets quite easily with tweezers, which is just as well, as they do need to be removed.

To make the Cream Sauce Base, pour the whipping cream into a non-stick pan, bring to the boil and reduce by about one-third to a coating consistency, as in Step 2, page 52.

Heat 50 g/2 oz of butter and half the oil in a large pan, and fry the onion and garlic until lightly browned. Add the mushrooms and fry until browned, then add the tomato, powdered bay leaf and thyme. Pour in the brandy, bring to the boil and simmer until the mixture dries out and begins to fry. Season to taste.

Heat the remaining oil in a hot frying pan and fry the fish livers (if using) for 10 seconds or less, then add them to the tomato mixture and scatter with the shredded basil leaves. Brush the fillets with oil, season, and place, skin-side uppermost, under a very hot grill until the skin is crispy but still red. Remove to a plate and keep warm.

Place the buttered bread under the hot grill and cook until crisp.

Pour the vermouth into the frying pan, bring to the boil and reduce by half. Add the fish stock and Cream Sauce Base and simmer until slightly thickened. Season, pour half into another small pan, then beat the remaining butter into the original pan. Set this creamy vermouth sauce aside, and keep warm until ready to serve.

Add the tomato mixture to the small pan and simmer until fairly dry, with no moisture running out.

Place the slices of toasted bread on heated dinner plates and spread with the tomato mixture. Lay the fillets on top of the mixture, garnish with the cream sauce and scatter with the remaining shredded basil.

Serves 6

Red Bream with a Sauce of Three Zests

6 fillets of red bream, about 125 g/4 oz each, skinned

seasoned flour

zest of 1 lime

zest of 1 lemon

zest of ½ orange

Cream Sauce Base, made from 300 ml/½ pint whipping cream

275 ml/9 fl oz white vermouth

75 g/5 oz butter

150 ml/¼ pint fish stock

salt and freshly ground black pepper

Filleted bream is usually sold already skinned as it has a rough skin that nobody would want to eat. However, the flesh itself is firm, with an excellent taste.

Dust the fillets lightly with the seasoned flour, shaking off any excess.

Remove the zests from the lime, lemon and the orange, using a zester, giving roughly equal quantities. Set aside about half of each colour for garnish.

To make the Cream Sauce Base, place the whipping cream in a non-stick pan, bring to the boil and reduce to a coating consistency, as in Step 2, page 52.

Place the remaining zests in a pan, add the vermouth and 25 g/1 oz of the butter. Bring to the boil and reduce until syrupy. Add the fish stock and Cream Sauce Base, bring to the boil and simmer for about 2 minutes. Season.

Heat 75 g/3 oz of the butter in a large, hot frying pan, and very quickly brown the fillets on both sides. Place the fish fillets on heated dinner plates, and keep warm. Strain the sauce into the frying pan, bring to the boil and correct the consistency if necessary. Season with plenty of pepper, then beat in the remaining 25 g/1 oz of butter, together with a squeeze of the lime juice.

To serve, pour the sauce around the fish and sprinkle over the remaining zests.

Serves 6

Note

The amount of stirring needed to thicken the cream depends on the age of the cream; the fresher it is, the more stirring is required.

Poached Turbot with a Creamy Crab Sauce

Another favourite recipe of mine for poached fish and one which will produce an impressive effect at a dinner party.

Turbot is a king of fishes – and according to that doyen of fish experts, Alan Davidson, one of the two finest flatfish in the world (the other being Dover sole).

Though a perfect foil for rich sauces, it can be a very expensive fish, so we poorer mortals could also achieve something of the same effect with this same sumptuous sauce, using poached fresh haddock or any other white fish.

For a special dinner party (and that's really when you would serve turbot) you can make the Crab Bisque from scratch. However, it freezes well, so it is worth making several batches and freezing some for use in this dish.

Make the Crab Bisque as described on page 102, bring to the boil and simmer until reduced to a concentrate. To make the Cream Sauce Base, add the cream to the Crab Bisque, bring to the boil and reduce to a coating consistency as in Step 2, page 52. Season with plenty of pepper and set aside.

Place the cutlets in a large pan, cover with milk and poach gently, without boiling, until done. Carefully lift the fish on to a plate, then gently remove the black skin and ease out the bones, leaving as much of the edge frill as possible. Keep the fish warm and add the juices to the sauce.

Reheat the sauce, and beat in the butter. To serve, place the fish on heated dinner plates, pour the sauce around, and garnish with pieces of crab meat or a small claw and pieces of blanched samphire, if using.

Serves 6

Cream Sauce Base, made from 150 ml/¼ pint whipping cream

300 ml/½ pint Crab Bisque (recipe on page 102)

6 turbot cutlets, about 275 g/9 oz each

about 300 ml/½ pint milk, to cover

50 g/2 oz butter

salt and freshly ground black pepper

To garnish (optional):
crab meat or crab claws, warmed

blanched samphire

Alternatively:
FRESH HADDOCK WITH A CREAMY CRAB SAUCE
Substitute 6 haddock fillets, skinned, about 175 g/6 oz each, folded in half, instead of the turbot cutlets. Proceed as in the main recipe.

Scallops in a Sauce of White Port, Lime and Ginger

25 g/1 oz fresh root ginger

175 ml/6 fl oz white port

zest and juice of 1 lime

Cream Sauce Base, made from 300 ml/½ pint whipping cream

15 scallops

50 g/2 oz butter

salt and freshly ground black pepper

sprigs of chervil, to garnish

GINGER, LIME AND PORT ICE-CREAM WITH LIME COULIS AND PISTACHIOS

Add 150 ml/¼ pint water and 2 tablespoons sugar to the ginger, lime and port, boil and reduce to about 75 ml/3 fl oz. Add 150 ml/¼ pint of the Cream Sauce Base, mix well, cool, strain and freeze. Serve with a lime syrup sauce (macerate zest of 1 lime in 150 ml/¼ pint Sugar Syrup Sauce Base for 30 minutes), chopped pistachio nuts and preserved lime leaves.

It is worth buying scallops in the shell for this dish. Rinse them quickly to get rid of mud and sand and dry immediately, or they absorb water and become bloated. The fishmonger can clean them for you, getting rid of the nasty bits, but ask him to give you the frill to make stock. Pickled ginger may be used instead of fresh root ginger – available from high quality delicatessens or oriental supermarkets.

To make the sauce, peel the ginger and slice into thin rounds. Pour the port into a saucepan, add the ginger and half the lime zest, bring to the boil and reduce to about 1 tablespoon to infuse the flavours. If more flavour is needed, add a little water and boil down again. Add the cream, season to taste, and set aside.

Ease the red coral from each scallop. Discard corals which are not plump and red, and prick the others carefully with a pin. Cut the white scallops crossways into penny shapes. Season with salt and pepper.

Heat the butter in a non-stick frying pan until it begins to darken, and cook the scallops for 10 seconds on one side, turn and repeat on the other side. Remove to a plate and keep warm. Toss the pricked corals in the hot pan for 5 seconds, and put them with the scallops.

Strain the sauce into the pan, bring to the boil and reduce to a light coating consistency (Step 2, page 52). Add a squeeze of fresh lime juice, and any juices from the scallops. Season to taste.

To serve, divide the scallop pieces between 6 heated starter plates. Pour the sauce around and garnish with lime zest, sprigs of chervil and corals.

Serves 6

Lobster with Vermouth Cream Sauce

1 cooked lobster,
about 750 g/1½ lb

For the sauce:
Cream Sauce Base, made from
300 ml/½ pint whipping cream

50 g/2 oz butter

75 g/3 oz shallots, chopped

150 ml/¼ pint white vermouth

40 g/1½ oz Parmesan
cheese, grated

1 good teaspoon
Dijon mustard

grated nutmeg

salt and freshly
ground black pepper

This sauce is wonderful with any cooked meat or fish but reaches its apogee with lobster. Raw lobster eggs, if available, can be pounded with butter and added to thicken and colour the sauce a delicate pink.

Allow half a lobster of this size per person, and cook it according to the instructions on page 108. It is always worth cooking the lobster yourself – very few fishmongers will do it as well, and you can be sure of its freshness.

The egg yolk glaze is my favourite way of finishing this sauce.

To make the Cream Sauce Base, pour the whipping cream into a non-stick pan, bring to the boil and reduce by about a third to a coating consistency, as in Step 2, page 52.

To make the sauce, heat the butter in a pan, add the shallots and cook gently until softened but not coloured, adding water if necessary. Add the vermouth, reduce to a syrup and then add 150 ml/¼ pint of water, the Cream Sauce Base and all the other sauce ingredients.

Bring to the boil and simmer for 10 minutes to draw out the flavours. If the sauce becomes too thick, add a little more water to return it to the right consistency.

Remove all the meat from the lobster, including the claws, and arrange in an oven-proof dish.

To make the glaze for the sauce, put the egg yolk and water in a heatproof bowl placed over simmering water, and whisk until foaming. Fold into the sauce, pour over the lobster and brown under a hot grill.
Serves 2

Scallop Quenelles in Smoked Butter Sauce

A delicious and unusual starter. However, it is easy to overpower the delicate taste of scallops with too much smoked haddock flavour. Only a little is required to give a suggestion of smokiness. Use the haddock poaching water in this recipe and reserve the fish itself for another use, such as Smoked Haddock Kedgeree on page 32. Make sure the scallops are fresh and dry (i.e. not soaked in water).

Clean all the scallops or persuade your fishmonger to do it for you; but in either case keep the trimmings to make the sauce (below). Place the large scallops and egg yolks in a liquidizer or food processor and purée until completely smooth. Add the double cream and season with salt and freshly ground black pepper.

Bring a large pan of water to the boil, reduce to a simmer and poach 12 quenelle-shaped tablespoons of the mixture in simmering water until firm (see method on page 58). Remove with a slotted spoon and place on a clean tea towel to drain.

To make the sauce, heat 25 g/1 oz of the butter in a pan, and cook the shallots until softened but not coloured. Add the white wine and reduce until syrupy. Add the scallop trimmings and fish stock or water, and poach to extract all the flavour. Strain and discard the solids. Add the whipping cream and reduce to a coating consistency, as in Step 2, page 52.

Meanwhile, bring the haddock water to the boil, add the queens, reduce the heat immediately, and remove the scallops as soon as they have whitened (just a few seconds). Set aside and keep warm. Reduce the haddock water to a concentrate.

Add the haddock water, bit by bit to the sauce, until the right, slightly smoky flavour is reached. If necessary, reduce again to reach a coating consistency. Beat in the remaining butter, taste and adjust the seasoning if necessary.

To serve, place 2 scallop quenelles on each heated starter plates, and spoon the sauce over. Garnish with sprigs of flat leaf parsley and the queen scallops.

Serves 6

9 scallops, about 250 g/8 oz

2 egg yolks

175 ml/6 fl oz double cream

salt and freshly
ground black pepper

For the sauce:
125 g/4 oz butter

25 g/1 oz shallots, chopped

150 ml/¼ pint white wine

Cream Sauce Base, made from
300 ml/½ pint whipping cream

300 ml/½ pint water from
poached smoked haddock

30 queen scallops

sprigs of flat leaf parsley,
to garnish

150 ml/¼ pint fish stock or water

Mussels with Saffron

A brilliant yellow dish, much enhanced by the green of the Swiss chard. It can be served as a main course or a starter.

A delicious alternative is to serve this dish, with the saffron sauce slightly thickened with a simple roux, as an accompaniment to poached monkfish or turbot (see the recipe below right).

To make the Cream Sauce Base, pour the whipping cream into a non-stick pan, bring to the boil and reduce to a coating consistency, as in Step 2, page 52.

To clean the mussels, rinse well in cold water and scrub off any mud or grit. Discard any with broken shells, and those which do not close immediately when tapped on the work surface.

Place them in a large pan and pour in the white wine. Cover, bring to the boil, shake the pan and simmer for a few minutes until all the shells have opened. Discard any which remain closed. When cool enough to handle, remove the mussels from their shells, pulling off the beards as you go. Strain the juices through muslin and reserve.

Arrange the mussels and chard in a large, ovenproof dish, or 6 small, individual dishes, reserving a few pieces of chard for garnish.

Pour half the reserved mussel juices into a saucepan, add the butter, saffron, thyme and bay leaf and bring to the boil, then simmer for about 5 minutes. Add the Cream Sauce Base, mix well, bring to the boil and reduce slightly to a coating consistency if necessary, topping up with the rest of the mussel juices if this doesn't make the sauce too salty. Remove the bay leaf, then set the sauce aside to keep warm.

Ten minutes before serving, beat the egg yolk and water together in a small bowl over a pan of simmering water until frothy. Fold into the sauce, taste and adjust the seasoning, then pour over the mussels. Add the chard garnish and place under a very hot grill until browned.

Serves 6

Cream Sauce Base, made from 600 ml/1 pint whipping cream

120 fresh mussels

150 ml/¼ pint white wine

250 g/8 oz Swiss chard leaves, green part only, torn and cooked

50 g/2 oz butter

1 large pinch of saffron threads

1 teaspoon chopped fresh thyme leaves

1 bay leaf

1 egg yolk

2 teaspoons water

salt and freshly ground black pepper

Alternatively:
MONKFISH OR TURBOT WITH MUSSELS AND A SAFFRON SAUCE
Poach 6 portions of monkfish or turbot in fish stock or court bouillon, and reserve. Place the fish on heated dinner plates, spoon the mussels beside and pour over the saffron sauce.

Normandy Chicken with Apples, Calvados and Cream

2 green dessert apples, such as Granny Smith

50 g/2 oz butter

2 small free-range chickens, jointed, (or chicken pieces for 6 people)

50 ml/2 fl oz Calvados

150 ml/¼ pint white wine

125 ml/4 fl oz well-flavoured chicken stock

Cream Sauce Base, made from 300 ml/½ pint whipping cream

salt and freshly ground black pepper

Alternatively:

NORMANDY PHEASANT

Substitute 2–3 jointed pheasants for the chicken, and French Golden Delicious apples for the Granny Smiths.

English Bramleys are not suitable as they cook down very quickly into a mush, whereas an eating variety will hold its shape. A red-skinned apple, or one of the striped red and gold kinds, cut into rounds and fried in butter, will produce a pretty alternative garnish.

The cooking of Normandy is typified by the use of apples, cider and Calvados – as well as butter and cream from the brown and white bespectacled cows of the region.

This recipe, more correctly known as Poulet Vallée d'Auge, is one of the great, classic dishes of Normandy, where it appears in as many versions as the Cornish Pasty does in the West Country of England. And of course every cook will assure you that theirs is the one-and-only authentic version!

Cut the apples into 8 segments each, remove the cores, but leave the skin on. Melt the butter in a large frying pan and fry the segments on both sides until browned. Remove and keep warm.

Place the chicken pieces in the pan with the skin sides down, and fry until well browned. Remove the pan from the heat, allow to cool slightly, return the apples to the pan, then pour in the Calvados and ignite. Shake the pan well until the flames die down.

Remove the chicken and apples, arrange on a serving dish, and set aside to keep warm.

Pour the white wine into the pan, bring to the boil and reduce until syrupy. Add the stock, return to the boil and reduce to 3 tablespoons Add the whipping cream, bring to the boil, and simmer until the sauce is reduced to a pouring consistency, as in Step 1, page 52.

Serve the chicken, garnished with apple segments, with the sauce poured over. Suitable accompaniments would include tiny boiled new potatoes and autumn vegetables such as sautéed Brussels sprouts and chestnuts, or tiny roasted parsnips.

Serves 6

Braised Chicken with Calvados and Crème Fraîche

Apple brandy used to be known as 'Apple Jack' but nowadays is more often described by its French name, Calvados. Distillation enhances the apple flavour and Calvados is now one of the most popular forms of alcohol used in the kitchen, complementing both sweet and savoury dishes equally.

The Cream Sauce Base can't, strictly speaking, be made from crème fraîche, but the delicious, lemony flavour of this slightly soured cream suits this dish so well that I have included this recipe in the Cream Sauce Base Section. Not entirely correct, but I hope you will enjoy it anyway.

Trim the celery hearts and cut into 6 pieces through the root. Heat the butter in a flameproof casserole, add the celery, onion and the white part of the leek, and cook gently until softened but not coloured. Add the herbs and clove, pour in the white wine, bring to the boil and simmer until syrupy. Add the Calvados and cook for a few minutes until the alcohol has boiled off.

Season the chicken inside and out with salt and freshly ground black pepper and tuck it into the middle of the vegetable mixture. Pour in the stock, bring to the boil and cover tightly. Lower the heat to a gentle simmer and cook the chicken for about 1–1½ hours, or until the juices run clear when you pierce a leg with a skewer. Remove the chicken, drain and set aside on a serving dish to keep warm.

Pour off some of the juices into a bowl, beat in the egg yolks and the crème fraîche.

Bring the rest of the cooking juices to the boil and reduce to about 150 ml/¼ pint. Strain out the herbs and clove, return the liquid to the pan and stir in the crème fraîche mixture. Heat until thickened, but do not boil. Taste and adjust the seasoning, pour around the chicken, and serve.

Serves 6

2 heads of young celery

25 g/1 oz butter

1 onion, sliced

2 young leeks, sliced

1 tablespoon chopped
fresh flat leaf parsley

1 bay leaf

l clove

150 ml/¼ pint white wine

50 ml/2 fl oz Calvados

1 plump chicken,
about 2 kg/4 lb

300 ml/½ pint chicken
or vegetable stock

4 egg yolks, beaten

150 ml/¼ pint crème fraîche

salt and freshly
ground black pepper

Chicken with a Cream and Paprika Archiduc Sauce

75 ml/3 fl oz groundnut oil

6 suprêmes of chicken

2 tablespoons brandy

3 shallots, chopped

300 ml/½ pint white wine

1 tablespoon paprika

4 tomatoes,
skinned and deseeded

2 sprigs of fresh tarragon

150 ml/¼ pint stock or water

Cream Sauce Base, made from
300 ml/½ pint whipping cream

salt and freshly
ground black pepper

To garnish:
1 red pepper

1 tablespoon groundnut oil

25 g/1 oz butter

500 g/1 lb fresh leaf
spinach, well washed

Archiduc is one of the classic French sauces, named after the Emperor of the Austro-Hungarian Empire (hence the paprika). Be sure to use good quality, fresh paprika for this colourful sauce – buy it in small quantities, keep it in the dark, and use it up quickly because, like most spices, it rapidly loses both flavour and colour.

Heat the oil in a large non-stick pan and fry the chicken pieces, on the skin side only, until lightly browned. Add the brandy and ignite. Shake the pan until the flames die down, then remove the chicken. Add the shallots and wine, bring to the boil and reduce until syrupy.

Stir in the paprika and cook for 2 minutes, then add the tomatoes, tarragon and stock or water. Replace the chicken, season with salt and pepper, cover and poach gently for 10–15 minutes, or until cooked through. Remove and keep warm.

To make the Cream Sauce Base, pour the whipping cream into a non-stick pan, bring to the boil and reduce to a coating consistency, as in Step 2, page 52.

To make the sauce, add the Cream Sauce Base to the juices in the pan and boil fiercely, stirring, for 2 minutes. Strain through a sieve into a clean pan, pushing through as much fibre as possible. Bring back to the boil and reduce to a fine coating consistency.

To make the garnish, cut the pepper in half, remove the seeds and place, skin-side up under a hot grill, or over a naked flame, until the skin blackens. Place in a plastic bag and set aside for a few minutes to loosen the skin. Remove from the bag, scrape off the skin and cut the flesh into strips. Heat the oil in a pan, cook the strips until soft, then drain on kitchen paper. Heat the butter in another pan and fry the washed spinach until wilted.

To serve, cut each chicken suprême crossways into 5 slices and place on heated dinner plates. Carefully spoon the sauce around and garnish with the spinach and red pepper slices.

Serves 6

Chicken in Creamed Curry Sauce

8 cardamom pods

125 ml/6 fl oz groundnut oil

1 medium onion, chopped

300 ml/½ pint white wine

3 tablespoons mild curry powder

4 tomatoes,
skinned and chopped

2.5 cm/1 inch fresh root
ginger, sliced but not skinned

150 ml/¼ pint chicken stock

6 chicken joints

Cream Sauce Base, made from
300 ml/½ pint whipping cream

salt and freshly
ground black pepper

Alternatively:
CREAMY
PRAWN CURRY
Substitute 500 g/1 lb cooked,
peeled prawns, omit the wine
and use cumin instead of
curry powder. Add the prawns
at the end, together with
1 tablespoon creamed coconut
thinned with 1 tablespoon
of water, and 1 tablespoon
of lemon juice, to acidulate.

Curry is a blanket word which covers thousands of different dishes. Use this as a basic recipe, and ring the changes by using different curry powders and spices. It can also be adapted to alternative main ingredients, such as lamb, or the prawns in the variation below left.

But don't expect – whatever you do – to end up with the flavour you'll find in authentic Indian cooking. This is a thoroughly Europeanized curry – you would never, for instance, find an Indian cook using wine in her dishes – and she would have no idea what you mean by 'curry powder'. She would grind her own spices into a garam masala, and the spices would vary according to the region she lived in and the dish she was cooking.

Open the cardamom pods and crush the seeds. Reserve.

Heat half the oil in a small pan, and simmer the onion until softened but not coloured. Add the white wine, bring to the boil and reduce until syrupy. Add the curry powder and raise the heat for a minute or so to release the flavours, stirring constantly to prevent it sticking and browning. Lower the heat and add the tomato, ginger, cardamom and stock. Simmer for 10 minutes to create a concentrated flavouring.

Heat the remaining oil in a frying pan and brown the chicken joints on the skin sides only. Season with some salt and freshly ground black pepper. Pour over the liquid, bring to the boil and simmer for about 20 minutes, until the chicken is tender. Remove and keep warm.

Add the cream to the pan juices and boil for about 2 minutes. Strain through a fine sieve into a clean pan, pushing through as much fibre as possible. Bring to the boil and reduce to a coating consistency, as in Step 2, page 52. Taste and adjust the seasoning.

Place the chicken pieces on a large serving dish, or heated dinner plates, pour over the sauce and serve with rice, poppadums, chutney, and sliced bananas with lemon and creamed coconut.
Serves 6

Chicken in a Sherry Sauce

A simple but delicious way of cooking chicken. It is very important to poach the suprêmes very gently, otherwise the meat will shrink and toughen.

Ideally, the poaching of tender cuts of poultry or fish should require the liquid to be maintained at a temperature above 75°C but below 100°C, which is boiling point. The meat then stays moist and tender. Boiling tightens the fibres, which toughens the meat.

I have included an absolutely delicious variation of this recipe, using fish – I would choose salmon, halibut, swordfish or perhaps snapper. Substitute fish stock instead of chicken stock of course, and try using white port instead of sherry – I find it goes very well with fish and seafood. I would serve both versions with baby new potatoes.

Melt the butter in a small pan and simmer the parsley, thyme, bay leaf, garlic and shallots for 10 minutes, adding a little water to prevent their browning.

When the shallots are transparent, add the wine, sherry and brandy, bring to the boil and reduce to a syrup.

Add the chicken stock and bring to the boil. Add the chicken suprêmes and poach them gently, with the liquid barely at a tremor for about 8–12 minutes, until cooked. Remove the chicken and place on heated dinner plates or a serving dish. Keep warm.

Bring the remaining liquid to the boil and reduce until syrupy. Add the whipping cream, bring back to the boil and simmer until reduced to a pouring consistency, as in Step 1, page 52.

Taste and adjust the seasoning, adding a squeeze of lemon juice if required. Strain the sauce, pour over the chicken suprêmes and serve immediately with boiled baby new potatoes, tossed in butter and sprinkled with snipped chives.

Serves 6

25 g/1 oz butter

1 tablespoon chopped
fresh flat leaf parsley

1 tablespoon chopped
fresh thyme leaves

1 bay leaf

1 clove garlic, sliced

6 shallots, chopped

1 tablespoon water

250 ml/8 fl oz white wine

125 ml/4 fl oz sherry

50 ml/2 fl oz brandy

300 ml/½ pint chicken stock

6 skinless chicken suprêmes

Cream Sauce Base, made from
300 ml/½ pint whipping cream

lemon juice, to taste

salt and freshly
ground black pepper

Alternatively:

POACHED FISH IN
WHITE PORT SAUCE
Poach 6 fish fillets or cutlets
for a few minutes in fish stock.
Substitute fish stock and white
port for chicken stock and
sherry, and proceed as in the
main recipe.

Peppered Steak

A delicious and very familiar steak recipe just perfect for ravenous people! Have your butcher cut the sizes you want and remember that the best rump steak comes from the smaller end.

As a variation, simmer the cooked steaks with the cream as it reduces, and do not sieve before serving – or substitute duck magrets (see the recipe below right).

Rub the steaks with the garlic, oil and half the peppercorns and leave in a plastic bag for up to 4 days in a refrigerator to tenderize and impregnate them with extra flavour.

When ready to cook, remove the steaks from the bag, and wipe off the excess marinade. Season with salt and press the remaining crushed peppercorns into the meat.

To make the Cream Sauce Base, pour the whipping cream into a non-stick pan, bring to the boil and reduce to a pouring consistency, as in Step 1, page 52.

Lightly oil a non-stick pan, and cook the steaks to the preferred degree of rareness. Remove, set aside, and keep warm.

Heat the pan until very hot and, well away from any flame, pour in the brandy and allow the alcohol to evaporate. Return to the heat, bring to the boil and reduce until syrupy. Pour in the stock, bring to the boil and reduce by half.

Add the Cream Sauce Base, bring to the boil and scrape up all the peppercorn bits. Reduce again to a mayonnaise-like emulsion, as in Step 3 on page 52 – but without allowing it to separate. Taste, adjust the seasoning and remove from the heat.

Place the steaks on heated dinner plates, pour over the cream-and-peppercorn sauce, and serve with steamed vegetables in season, such as broad beans and, of course, sauté potatoes.

Serves 6

6 rump steaks

2 cloves garlic, crushed

1 tablespoon groundnut oil

20 whole black peppercorns, crushed

Cream Sauce Base, made from 450 ml/¾ pint whipping cream

150 ml/¼ pint good brandy

150 ml/¼ pint beef stock

salt

Alternatively:

DUCK MAGRETS WITH GARLIC AND GREEN PEPPERCORNS

Brush 6 duck breasts, prick the skin all over, rub with crushed garlic, and press in some green peppercorns. Brown in a hot, non-stick pan, skin-side down, to draw out as much fat as possible, which must then be discarded. This will take about 8 minutes. Turn the breasts over and place in a preheated oven at 150°C (300°F) Gas Mark 2 for 15 minutes, to finish cooking and rest. Proceed with the sauce, substituting a duck or chicken stock, and reduce to a coating consistency. Spoon the sauce on to dinner plates, carve the duck and lay the slices on top.

Veal with Mozzarella and Sage, wrapped in Parma Ham

175 g/6 oz mozzarella cheese

6 veal slices from
best end of loin

6 slices Parma ham

6 fresh sage leaves

50 g/2 oz butter

150 ml/¼ pint
dry Italian white wine

150 ml/¼ pint chicken
or veal stock

Cream Sauce Base, made from
150 ml/¼ pint whipping cream

50 g/2 oz Parmesan
cheese, grated

freshly ground black pepper

Alternatively:
CHICKEN BIRDS
Replace the veal slices with chicken breasts. Place the chicken between 2 sheets of clingfilm and pound with a rolling pin until flattened. Proceed as in the main recipe and serve with Lyonnaise potatoes and a crisp salad of mixed leaves.

A thoroughly traditional veal dish, made much more delicious with a Cream Sauce Base. The perfect accompaniment is steamed French beans, or perhaps mangetout.

In Italy, this dish is known as 'involtini', and to the French 'paupiettes'. The old-fashioned English name for this dish was veal olives or veal birds. You could also substitute thin slices of minute steak, in which case the dish is known as beef olives.

Cut the mozzarella into 6 fingers. Using a meat bat or rolling pin, beat the veal slices to flatten them and break up the fibres (which would otherwise make them twist and curl as they cook).

Place the slices of veal on a board and lay a slice of ham on each one. Roll a sage leaf around each 'finger' of cheese, place it at one end of a slice of veal, roll up the meat and anchor with two cocktail sticks. Repeat with the other 5 pieces of veal.

Heat the butter in a pan until it froths. Add the veal rolls and cook on the flatter side only until browned. Lay them in an ovenproof dish, cooked side up. Keep warm.

Pour the wine into the hot pan and reduce until syrupy. Add the stock, scraping in any browned, fried bits from the veal, then pour in the cream. Bring to the boil and reduce to a pouring consistency, as in Step 1, page 52. Season with plenty of freshly ground black pepper, then pour over the veal. Sprinkle with the Parmesan cheese and place in a preheated oven at 180°C (350°F) Gas Mark 4 and cook until brown and bubbling.

Serves 6

Ragoût of Veal with a Creamy Sauce

This creamy veal stew takes me back to childhood. I think I must have been given it first as 'comfort food' after a bout of measles or some other illness and I love it. Nursery but nice!

Heat 50 g/2 oz of the butter in a large pan and sauté the onions, the celery and veal until all the liquid has evaporated. Add the herbs and lemon zest and cover with chicken stock. Bring to the boil, season and simmer for 1½ hours or until the veal is cooked.

Strain off the liquid into a clean pan, bring to the boil and reduce to 900 ml/1½ pints.

To make the Cream Sauce Base, pour the whipping cream into a non-stick pan, bring to the boil and reduce to a pouring consistency, as in Step 1, page 52. Add to the reduced cooking liquid and mix well.

In a clean bowl, mix the egg yolks with the cornflour then pour in some of the hot liquid. Mix well and return to the pan. Bring the sauce almost to boiling point, stirring continuously. Add the cooked veal (discarding the lemon zest, onions, celery and herbs if preferred).

Heat the remaining butter in a small frying pan, add the button mushrooms, sauté gently for a few minutes, then add a squeeze of lemon juice.

Heap the creamy veal on to a heated serving plate or 6 dinner plates, garnish with the button mushrooms and serve.

Serves 6

75 g/3 oz butter

2 onions, chopped

2 celery stalks, chopped

1.5 kg/3 lb stewing veal, cut into bite-sized pieces

1 bay leaf

1 tablespoon chopped fresh thyme leaves

1 tablespoon chopped fresh rosemary leaves

grated zest and juice of 1 lemon

1.2 litres/2 pints chicken stock

Cream Sauce Base, made from 175 ml/6 fl oz whipping cream

3 egg yolks

1 teaspoon cornflour

salt and freshly ground black pepper

250 g/8 oz whole button mushrooms, to garnish

Pork Medallions with Apples, Calvados and Wild Rice

3 pork fillets, trimmed and sliced into small medallions

about 500 g/1 lb long-grain rice, or a mixture of long-grain and wild rice, boiled, for 6 people

Cream Sauce Base, made from 450 ml/¾ pint whipping cream

18 baby leeks

about 1 tablespoon groundnut oil

50 g/2 oz butter

3 sweet red apples, unpeeled and sliced into segments

6 tablespoons Calvados

75 ml/3 fl oz balsamic vinegar

300 ml/½ pint light stock (chicken, veal or vegetable)

¼ teaspoon paprika, plus extra, to garnish

soy sauce, to taste

salt and freshly ground black pepper

Cooking the pork medallions on skewers will help to prevent the meat from becoming overdone and drying out. Serve the pork 'en brochette' if you like, or remove the skewers as illustrated. If using wooden skewers, don't forget to soak them first.

Season the pork fillets, boil the rice in the usual way and set aside.

To make the Cream Sauce Base, pour the cream into a non-stick pan, bring to the boil and reduce to a pouring consistency, as in Step 1, page 52

Place the leeks in a pan, cover with salted water, bring to the boil, reduce the heat and simmer until done. Drain, but reserve some of the cooking liquid. Set aside the leeks and keep warm.

Brush a very hot non-stick pan with the oil and quickly brown the pork medallions, 6 at a time (do not attempt to cook them through).

Heat the butter in a small pan and fry the apple segments until browned and slightly softened. Pour over the Calvados and reduce until syrupy. Remove the apple slices and thread on to the skewers, alternately with the pork medallions

Add the balsamic vinegar to the hot pan, then pour in the stock, leek water, and Cream Sauce Base, then season with paprika and soy sauce. Bring to the boil to thicken a little.

Place the skewers of apple and pork medallions in the pan, adding any juices. Continue to simmer the sauce and baste the skewers, until the meat is cooked and lightly coated.

Serve the pork on heated dinner plates, add the poached leeks, pour over the sauce and sprinkle with a little extra paprika. Garnish with the apple slices and serve with boiled long-grain rice, or a mixture of long-grain and wild rice.

Serves 6

Pickled Pork

10 cardamom pods

12 juniper berries, pickled

1.5 kg/1½ lb
pickled belly of pork

2 kg/4 lb broad beans,
in the pod

125 g/4 oz salted butter

6 mint leaves, or to taste

350 ml/12 fl oz crème fraîche

1 teaspoon Dijon mustard

freshly ground black pepper

The broad beans absolutely make this recipe, counterbalancing what would otherwise be a rather rich dish. I would always use fresh broad beans, but, you could substitute mushy peas.

This dish approaches the Cream Sauce Base in a different way from most of the other recipes in this section. Rather than reducing whipping cream, I have added lovely, lemony crème fraîche at the end instead, which helps to point up the special flavour of pickled pork. It isn't strictly correct, but it is certainly delicious!

You should order half a pickled belly of pork, rib end, as lean as possible, at least ten days in advance.

Open the cardamom pods and extract the seeds. Place the seeds and juniper berries in a spice mill or coffee grinder, and grind to a purée.

Bone the pickled belly of pork. Sprinkle the underside of the pork with the cardamom and juniper mixture. Roll the piece up lengthways, tie it in several places, place in a deep flameproof casserole or pan and cover with cold water. Bring to the boil, reduce the heat and simmer gently for 2 hours. Lift out and cut off the skin.

Meanwhile, shell the broad beans, and cook in boiling salted water until soft. Drain and place in a liquidizer or food processor. Add the butter, mint leaves and lots of freshly ground black pepper and work briefly to a mush. Set aside and keep warm.

Ladle 150 ml/¼ pint of the pork cooking liquid into a saucepan, bring to the boil and reduce to 2 tablespoons. Stir the crème fraîche, add the mustard and pour into a hot sauceboat.

To serve, spoon the broad beans on to a large heated serving dish, or 6 dinner plates, cut the pork into thick rounds and lay them on top, with the mint and mustard sauce served separately.

Serves 6

Lamb Cutlets à l'Anglaise

Dipping meat and fish into egg and breadcrumbs and frying is a method known as 'à l'Anglaise' by the French and – it must be admitted – in a rather derogatory tone. Nevertheless, it is still a delicious method of cooking – the interior stays juicy and the meat or fish ration goes much further. Try it also with scallops - or even a thin piece of steak. Use a high temperature, then drain under a grill. The fun of this dish is in the accompanying sauces – this is one of my favourites, but you could substitute others from this book, such as Onion Confit on page 164, Hot Tomato Sauce on page 165, and the unusual sour-sweet sauce with the Veal Kidneys on page 166.

Place the onions in a saucepan, cover with water, bring to the boil and simmer for 5 minutes until tender. Drain well. When cool enough to handle, cut off the roots and squeeze the shoot ends so the edible part slips out of the skin. (You may need to tweak them a bit.)

Trim the chine bone off the cutlets and remove as much fat as you choose. Scrape the end of the bones for easy handling.

Place the breadcrumbs on a flat plate. Beat the eggs, and dip the cutlets first in the egg mixture, then in the breadcrumbs until well coated. Heat half the butter in a frying pan and fry the cutlets on both sides. Keep warm and crisp under a gentle grill, turning occasionally while you prepare the sauce.

To make the Cream Sauce Base, pour the whipping cream into a non-stick pan, bring to the boil and reduce to a pouring consistency, as in Step 1, page 52.

Heat the remaining butter in a pan and sauté the button mushrooms for a few minutes until lightly browned. Add the white wine, bring to the boil and reduce until syrupy.

Add the salami, the small onions, paprika and Cream Sauce Base, bring to the boil, reduce to a coating consistency again, then stir in the chives. Taste and adjust the seasoning.

Divide the sauce between heated dinner plates, place the cutlets on top and serve with hot buttered noodles.

Serves 6

18 baby onions, unpeeled

12 lamb cutlets

125 g/4 oz fresh white breadcrumbs

3 eggs

50 g/2 oz butter, preferably clarified

Cream Sauce Base, made from 150 ml/¼ pint whipping cream

125 g/4 oz button mushrooms, quartered

150 ml/¼ pint white wine

125 g/4 oz sliced salami, cut into ribbons

1 teaspoon paprika

1 tablespoon chopped fresh chives

salt and freshly ground black pepper

Roast Saddle of Hare in a Creamy Sauce

It's most unusual to have a cream sauce to go (and go very well indeed) with an underdone roast. Serve with a creamy purée of cooked fresh chestnuts.

Trim back the ribs on the saddles with kitchen scissors so that they sit flat. Each saddle is covered with two layers of gristly skin and both must be freed to prevent the meat curling up when cooked. So, with the pointed end of a knife, insert the blade at the tail end, just under the first thick membrane, with the blunt side towards the backbone. Push it as far towards the neck as you can without damaging the meat underneath and saw gently with the knife, pushing outward towards the cut rib ends. Leave the membrane attached along the backbone. Do the same on the other side. Now gently cut the second layer of gristle off the meat using the same method.

To make a hare stock, add the hare trimmings to the chicken stock, bring to the boil and simmer until reduced by half. Strain.

Mix the marinade ingredients together in a jug. Place the meat in a roasting dish and pour over the marinade. Set aside for at least 1 hour. (Alternatively, place saddles and marinade in a plastic bag, gently knead the marinade into the meat, and set aside for 1 hour.) When ready to cook, cover the dish with foil and roast in a preheated oven at 220°C (425°F) Gas Mark 7 for about 20 minutes.

Remove from the oven, place on a carving board, make two long cuts, either side of the backbone, and remove the meat whole from the rib cage. Turn over and remove the two tiny fillets from underneath. Keep all the meat warm and add the juices to the hare stock.

To make the Cream Sauce Base, pour the cream into a non-stick pan, bring to the boil and reduce to a coating consistency, as in Step 2, page 52. Add to the hare stock and grind in lots of black pepper. Season, bring to the boil, and reduce to a thin cream.

To serve, divide the sauce between heated dinner plates. Slice the meat lengthways into strips and lay flat on top of the sauce. Suitable accompaniments should include a purée of fresh chestnuts (see page 152), sautéed spinach or steamed romanesco, and mashed potatoes.

Serves 6

2 saddles of hare

600 ml/1 pint chicken stock

Cream Sauce Base, made from 450 ml/¾ pint whipping cream

salt and freshly ground black pepper

For the marinade:
150 ml/¼ pint Marc de Bourgogne, grappa or brandy

300 ml/½ pint water

Note:
BUYING HARE
When buying a hare, make sure the butcher does not cut the saddle in half across the waist. You need a whole saddle from neck to legs for this dish, as it is carved lengthways, parallel to the backbone.
It may be necessary to order the hare in advance. Ask for the blood if you want to make a proper hare stew later. One large hare will feed 3 people from the saddle, and the legs another 3 using the recipe for Hare in Red Wine on page 150. So, in the end, it's not as expensive as it might otherwise be.

Brown Sugar Parfait with Prunes and Amaretti

40 g/1½ oz soft brown sugar

Cream Sauce Base, made from 300 ml/½ pint whipping cream

250 g/8 oz no-need-to-soak prunes, roughly chopped

1 dozen amaretti biscuits

6 marrons glacé (optional)

Place the sugar and cream in a non-stick pan, bring to the boil and reduce to a coating consistency, as in Step 2, page 52.

Mix in the prunes and marrons, then spoon the mixture into glasses and chill. Crumble the amaretti biscuits over the top and serve.

Serves 6

Ginger Baked Custard

5 egg yolks

6 pieces of stem ginger

1 tablespoon of ginger syrup

Cream Sauce Base, made from 750 ml/1¼ pints whipping cream

Alternatively:
GINGER
CRÈME BRÛLÉE
Make the Ginger Baked Custard as in the main recipe. Cook the Sugar Syrup Sauce Base (page 156) longer until it forms a caramel, then pour out on to a sheet of foil. When cool and set, break into fine crumbs and sprinkle over the top.

This is an unusual and very simple version of baked custard, not overly sweet, but packed with zingy flavour. The variation below left is a pretend crème brûlée.

Place the egg yolks, the stem ginger and the syrup from the bottle of ginger into a liquidizer or food processor and blend until smooth.

To make the Cream Sauce Base, pour the whipping cream into a non-stick pan, bring to the boil and reduce to a pouring consistency, as in Step 1, page 52.

Pour the sauce base on to the egg mixture in the liquidizer, with the motor running.

Pour into 6 cocotte dishes and bake in a preheated oven for about 20–25 minutes, at 140°C (275°F) Gas Mark 1 until set.

Serves 6

Sponge Pudding with a Saffron Cream Sauce

A whole range of creamy dessert sauces can be made using a puréed fruit or coulis as the basic flavouring. This sauce recipe uses tomato as the fruit (which of course it is, technically) – and the flavour is tantalizingly difficult to recognize.

I have teamed it here with a traditional Sponge Pudding, but you could use the same sauce with many other dessert dishes, such as poached pears or ice-cream.

To make the Saffron Cream Sauce, pour 2–3 tablespoons of boiling water over the saffron threads and set aside until all the colour has been extracted from the strands (or soak overnight). If using powder, soak for 5–10 minutes in boiling water. Use the liquid as well as the strands or powder in the recipe.

Heat the oil in a pan, add the thyme, tarragon and tomatoes, bring to the boil and cook to a pulp. Add the wine, bring to the boil and reduce until syrupy. Add the sugar syrup and saffron, and simmer for 10 minutes.

Pour the whipping cream into a non-stick pan, bring to the boil and reduce to a pouring consistency, as in Step 1, page 52. Add to the tomato mixture, bring to the boil, strain and check for sweetness and texture. It should still be a pouring consistency. Pour into a sauceboat and keep warm.

To make the Sponge Pudding, beat the butter and sugar together in a bowl, then beat in the eggs and fold in the flour and orange zest.

Turn the mixture into a greased pudding basin, cover with foil and cook in a preheated oven at 190°C (375°F) Gas Mark 5 for about 45 minutes. Turn out of the basin on to a heated serving dish. Serve accompanied by the Saffron Sauce.

Serves 6

big pinch of saffron threads
or 1 packet of saffron powder

25 ml/1 fl oz grapeseed oil

1 teaspoon chopped
fresh thyme leaves

1 tablespoon chopped fresh
tarragon leaves

about 375 g/12 oz canned Italian
plum tomatoes, chopped

150 ml/¼ pint white wine

Sugar Syrup Sauce Base,
to taste (see page 156)

Cream Sauce Base, made from
450 ml/¾ pint whipping cream

For the sponge pudding:
125 g/4 oz butter

125 g/4 oz sugar

2 eggs

125 g/4 oz self-raising flour

a little grated orange zest

brown
SAUCE BASE

THIS SECTION SHOULD almost be a book in itself. Unlike Egg, Cream or Sugar Sauces, which will take only a matter of minutes, this one has to be made up from multiple ingredients and the quality of the base often depends on the care taken in their preparation.

There are NO suitable substitutes to be found on the supermarket shelves. The actual technique is not difficult but, although it can be prepared days or even months in advance, it cannot be satisfactorily made instantly.

The Brown Sauce Base is the result of long, slow cooking, either for several hours in a very low oven or on top of the stove – or overnight in a slow cooker.

However, though this sauce base takes a long time to cook, it takes just few minutes to prepare, and is, in essence, a classic *Sauce Espagnole*.

It can also be the basis of many other classic sauces – the simple addition of white wine, red wine or Madeira results in the three different families of classic sauces, as you will see from the chart on page 99.

So – to make Brown Sauce Base, first make a good Brown Meat Stock as described on page 101. Then follow the step-by-step photographs overleaf to produce the Brown Sauce Base. The base may then be frozen for use in any of the dishes in this chapter.

1 Heat half the groundnut oil in a small frying pan, add the flour and cook, stirring, until nicely browned. Set aside.

3 Finely chop the tomatoes, add to the vegetables in the pan. The mixture will become very liquid, then dry out later. Fry until brown.

BROWN SAUCE BASE

50 ml/2 fl oz groundnut oil

25 g/1 oz flour

500 g/1 lb onions

500 g/1 lb carrots

2 celery sticks

1 large leek

125 g/4 oz mushrooms or mushroom peelings

500 g/1 lb ripe tomatoes

1.5–3 litres/4–5 pints
Brown Meat Stock (page 101)

25 g/1 oz cornflour mixed with about 1 cup of cold water per 600 ml/1 pint of liquid

2 Using a separate pan, heat the remaining oil, finely chop all the vegetables (except the tomatoes) and fry until brown.

4 When the tomato mixture has dried out, add the browned flour to the pan of vegetables and stir well.

5 Add the Brown Meat Stock (recipe on page 101), bring to the boil and simmer gently for about 2 hours (or overnight in a slow cooker).

STEP-BY-STEP METHOD

1 Heat half the groundnut oil in a small pan, add the flour, and cook, stirring, until browned.

2 Finely chop the onions, carrots, celery, leek and mushrooms. Heat the remaining oil in a separate pan, add all the vegetables (except the tomatoes) and fry until brown (about 10 minutes). Take care not to burn the onions at this stage.

3 Finely chop the tomatoes, add to the vegetables in the pan. The tomatoes will first throw out a good deal of liquid, which will slowly evaporate, then the sugars will start to caramelize. Fry until brown.

4 Add the browned flour to the browned vegetables in the pan and stir well.

5 Add the Brown Meat Stock (see page 101), bring to the boil and simmer on top of the stove or in the oven for 2 hours, or overnight in a slow cooker.

6 Add 600 ml/1 pint of cold water to the pan to bring the quantity of liquid back to the original level. Bring to the boil on top of the stove.   (cont.)

6 Add 600 ml/1 pint of cold water to the pan to bring the quantity back to the original level. Bring back to the boil on top of the stove.

7 Strain through a sieve into a pan, shaking gently to extract all the liquid. Do not push the vegetables through the sieve.

8 Mix 1 tablespoon of cornflour with about 1 cup of water, and add the mixture to the strained stock in the pan, whisking constantly.

9 Return the mixture to the boil, then simmer gently for about 30 minutes until reduced to 1–1.2 litres/1¾–2 pints.

STEP-BY-STEP METHOD (continued)

7 Strain through a sieve into a pan, shaking the sieve gently to extract all the liquid. Do not push the vegetables through.

8 Mix 1 tablespoon of cornflour in 1 cup of cold water and add to the pan, whisking.

9 Return the mixture to the boil, then simmer for 30 minutes, until reduced to 1–1.2 litres/1¾–2 pints. The thickening qualities of the flour will be dissipated over this long cooking time, and becomes part of the sauce texture, rather than a thickener.

FREEZING BROWN SAUCE BASE

It is worthwhile making a large quantity of Brown Sauce Base. Feel free to multiply the ingredients by two or three. In fact, the size of your pot is the only limitation. When complete, cool and chill. The Brown Sauce Base will set. Cut it into convenient sections, such as 150 ml/¼ pint or 300 ml/½ pint each, and freeze for later use. Thaw in the usual way.

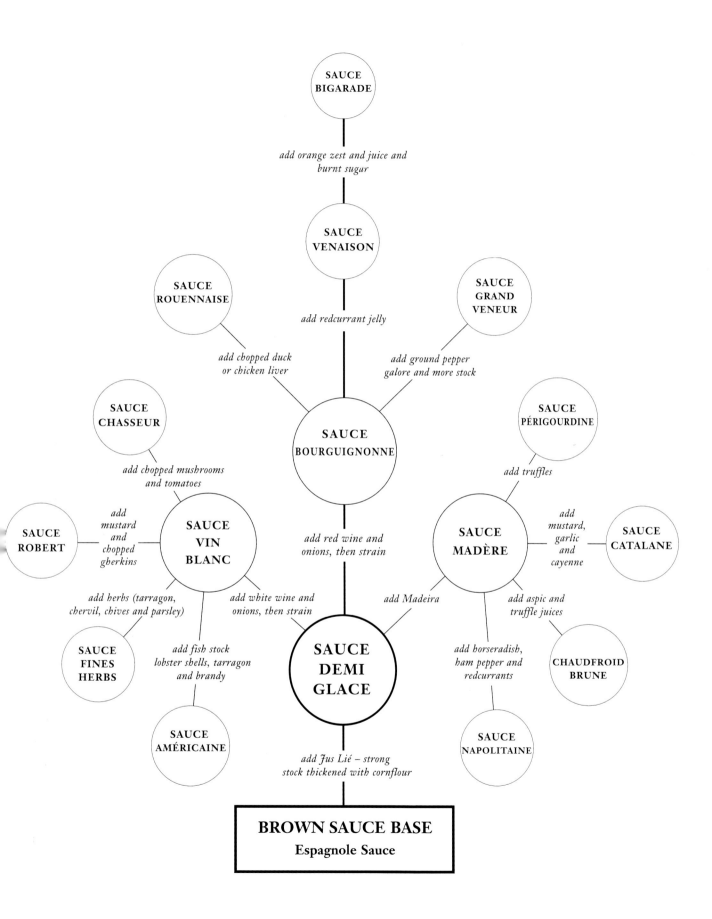

SAUCE
BIGARADE

*add orange zest and juice and
burnt sugar*

SAUCE
VENAISON

SAUCE
ROUENNAISE

SAUCE
GRAND
VENEUR

add redcurrant jelly

*add chopped duck
or chicken liver*

*add ground pepper
galore and more stock*

SAUCE
CHASSEUR

SAUCE
PÉRIGOURDINE

*add chopped mushrooms
and tomatoes*

add truffles

SAUCE
ROBERT

*add
mustard
and
chopped
gherkins*

SAUCE
VIN
BLANC

SAUCE
BOURGUIGNONNE

*add red wine and
onions, then strain*

SAUCE
MADÈRE

*add
mustard,
garlic
and
cayenne*

SAUCE
CATALANE

*add herbs (tarragon,
chervil, chives and parsley)*

*add white wine and
onions, then strain*

add Madeira

*add aspic and
truffle juices*

SAUCE
FINES
HERBS

*add fish stock
lobster shells, tarragon
and brandy*

SAUCE
DEMI
GLACE

*add horseradish,
ham pepper and
redcurrants*

CHAUDFROID
BRUNE

SAUCE
AMÉRICAINE

*add Jus Lié – strong
stock thickened with cornflour*

SAUCE
NAPOLITAINE

BROWN SAUCE BASE
Espagnole Sauce

Making Stocks

Good cooking is always very much easier with homemade stocks. Make them often, so their preparation will become just a simple matter of routine – almost a habit. Store in the deep freeze. If you keep them in the refrigerator, you must boil them up every 2 days.

The easiest way to make poultry, game or meat stocks is in a slow cooker. Every night or so, as needed, all carcasses, onion peelings (not the root), carrots, bones from the joint, etc., are put into a stockpot, covered with boiling water, brought to a gentle boil for about 10 minutes to cook any vegetables (since vegetables do not cook below boiling point), then simmered overnight.

The following day, strain out the bones and discard, then chill the resulting stock, remove the fat and boil down the stock to a concentrated juice, which can then be frozen and stored.

This sort of stock making is invaluable. However, it produces what is known as a 'white' stock: that is, none of the sugar in the protein or vegetable has been caramelized.

To make the best-quality Brown Meat Stock, the ingredients are browned first, these sugars are caramelized, giving the stock a much richer colour and a little more flavour. Making this type of stock is more of a bind but, combined with another activity which can be interrupted, like ironing or television (to each his own pleasures!) it becomes an entertainment.

Brown Stock is usually made in large quantities, and therefore less often, but it does need a bit of forethought. However, the amount of food wastage in ordinary households is enormous – start making stocks and you'll be amazed how much you save!

All the recipes in this chapter use Brown Sauce Base made with the Brown Meat Stock recipe opposite. To emphasize the true flavour of a particular meat, game or poultry, make the Sauce Base with one of the stock recipes below. Fish Stock is not used in a Brown Sauce Base, but is included for reference.

CHICKEN STOCK
Make chicken stock using 5 kg/10 lb of chicken and/or chicken bones, as well as the vegetables and herbs as listed in the recipe opposite for Brown Meat Stock. Brown the bones in the oven first, and proceed as in the recipe opposite.

DUCK OR GAME STOCK
Substitute 5 kg/10 lb of duck or game meat and bones, and proceed as for chicken stock.

LAMB, PORK OR VEAL STOCK
Substitute 5 kg/10 lb lamb, pork or veal bones. Veal makes the richest stock. Lamb or pork stock is rather sweet, so use in small quantities.

FISH STOCK
Wash 5 kg/10 lb heads and bones of non-oily fish under running water and remove the gills and bloody bits with scissors. Finely chop 500 g/1 lb onions, 500 g/1 lb carrots, 2 celery sticks, 1 leek and 2–3 outer leaves of fennel. Fry in a little groundnut oil, but do not brown. Place in a large saucepan with the trimmed fish, 20 peppercorns, 2 sprigs of thyme, 2 bay leaves, cover with water, bring to the boil and simmer for 20 minutes. Strain, reserve the liquid and discard the solids. Allow the liquid to settle, then pour off the clear stock on top and reserve. Discard the rest.

Brown Meat Stock

This stock is the basis of the Brown Sauce Base used here. Collect meat trimmings and bones, or order them from your butcher. Use rib bones, not marrow bones – which I think only add fat, not flavour. Include mostly beef and veal, but very few pork or lamb, because they will make the stock very sweet. Omit potatoes, cabbage, swedes, turnips, parsnips or cold cooked meats as these cloud the stock or turn sour with long cooking. You could include some shin of beef or a boiling chicken and serve as a separate dish.

about 5 kg/10 lb bones, e.g. beef, veal and other mixed bones
fresh meat, such as meat trimmings, a boiling fowl, some shin of beef or cheek
500 g/1 lb carrots
1.5 kg/3 lb onions
2 celery sticks or trimmings (not the leaves)
3 leeks
1 kg/2 lb fresh tomatoes, or
about 750 g/1½ lb tinned tomatoes
1 bay leaf
2 sprigs of thyme
a few parsley stalks

Place the bones in a roasting tin and cook in a preheated oven at about 190°C (375°F) Gas Mark 5 until the fat and juices run and the meat browns.

Remove the bones to a large stockpot. Place the tin on top of the stove, add the vegetables and gently fry until nicely browned, but do not burn. The juices must caramelize, or the effect will be of a 'white' stock rather than brown. Add the browned vegetables to the stockpot. Cover with cold water, skim any scum, heat gently to boiling point, reduce the heat and simmer up to 8 hours.

If your stockpot has a tap, draw off all the clear stock, leaving the fat behind. Otherwise, remove the bones, strain the stock and chill overnight. Remove the fat from the top and discard.

Bring to the boil in a saucepan and reduce to the desired depth of flavour – you should have about 3 litres/5 pints. You can also reduce to about 600 ml/1 pint of concentrate for storing.

POINTS TO REMEMBER

There are a few guidelines which will help you to achieve good, clear stock every time.

1 Bring the stock to the boil, then reduce to a simmer. Never continue to boil a stock after it has reached boiling point. It should be just hot enough for the steam to find a blowhole in the fat on top and puff gently through it.

2 If you do let it boil again, the fat on the surface will be drawn down into the body of the stock. There it will gradually combine and emulsify with the liquid, resulting in an opaque and unpleasantly fatty-tasting stock.

3 Collect suitable bones and meat trimmings and keep them in the freezer.

4 You can also order them from your butcher. Ask for plenty of beef rib bones, not marrow bones, as the traditionalists insist. Too many lamb or pork bones will make the stock too sweet.

5 Never add salt to the stock – otherwise any of the dishes you make from it will be too salty.

Crab Bisque

25 ml/1 fl oz olive oil

2 shallots, chopped

2 cloves garlic, chopped

300 ml/½ pint medium
dry white wine

300 ml/½ pint
Brown Sauce Base

300 ml/½ pint fish stock

1 hen crab,
about 1 kg/2 lb, cooked

50 g/2 oz rice

½ tablespoon freshly
chopped tarragon leaves

1 baguette loaf, sliced
into rounds, (12 slices)

butter, for spreading

salt and lots of freshly
ground black pepper

To garnish:

6 tablespoons crème fraîche

6 sprigs of tarragon

A wonderful, satisfying and extraordinary soup that tastes gorgeous – and remarkable in that it is so unlike lobster bisque.

The surprise is that it is made from a Brown Sauce Base – which is so completely unexpected for a fish recipe.

This bisque is very versatile. Make extra (it freezes well) and use in recipes such as Poached Turbot in a Creamy Crab Sauce on page 69 and the Soufflé of Sole Quenelles on page 107.

To make the soup base, heat the olive oil in a large saucepan, and fry the shallots and garlic until softened but not coloured. Pour in the white wine, bring to the boil and reduce until syrupy. Add the Brown Sauce Base and fish stock and mix well.

Remove the big claws from the crab, and reserve for garnish. Clean the crab by removing the stomach and dead men's fingers. Separate the white meat and reserve. Chop up the rest, including the shell, into small pieces, then place in the saucepan with the soup base, stir well, bring to the boil, cover and simmer for about 30–40 minutes.

In a separate pan, cook the rice in 250 ml/8 fl oz of water for at least 25 minutes or more, to make it soft and sloppy.

Strain the soup through a colander, and then through a sieve to remove all traces of shell. Pour the soup into a liquidizer or food processor, together with enough cooked rice to thicken it, then blend until smooth.

Pour the soup into a rinsed-out pan, add the chopped tarragon, lots of freshly ground black pepper and some salt. Heat through, taste, and adjust the seasoning.

Butter the bread slices on one side and toast in the oven.

Place 1 tablespoon of the reserved white crab meat on to each slice of toast. Ladle the soup into individual heated soup bowls and swirl 1 tablespoon of crème fraîche into each. Float 1–2 slices of crab-topped toast on top of each serving, garnish with the sprigs of tarragon, and serve.

Serves 6

Brown Onion Soup

Making a soup using the Brown Sauce Base takes just a matter of minutes. The frying medium used in browning the onions will flavour the final result, so you should use a flavourless oil such as groundnut if you want only the onion flavour to predominate. If you would like to use bacon fat as a variation, this will give the soup a delicious flavour too.

The depth of 'brown-ness' you achieve when browning the onions will also flavour the soup accordingly.

Heat the oil in a large pan, and fry the onions gently until coloured to the degree you require for flavour – make sure you achieve at least a golden, caramel colour.

Add the water to the Brown Sauce Base, stir well, and pour over the onions. Simmer for 20 minutes, then bring to the boil and reduce the liquid to 1.5 litres/2½ pints to concentrate the flavour. Taste and adjust the seasoning.

Toast the slices of bread, then pile the cheese on top and place them under the grill or in a hot oven until the cheese has melted.

Pour the soup into heated soup bowls, and float the toasted cheese rounds on top.

Serves 6

about 2 tablespoons groundnut oil

3 large onions, sliced into rings

900 ml/1½ pints **Brown Sauce Base**

900 ml/1½ pints water

1–1½ baguette loaves, cut into rounds (18 slices)

125 g/4 oz grated cheese

salt and freshly ground black pepper

Garlic Soup

Place the unpeeled cloves of garlic in a saucepan, cover with cold water, bring to the boil and simmer for about 20 minutes. Remove the garlic, but retain the water. Peel the garlic and discard the skins, then return the cloves to the water. Add the Brown Sauce Base.

Simmer for 1 hour or more, then place in a liquidizer or food processor and purée until smooth. Add the milk, then top up to about 1.5 litres/2½ pints with water. Bring to just below boiling point, and season well with salt and freshly ground black pepper.

Serve in heated soup plates and sprinkle liberally with Parmesan, or roll hot croûtons in grated Parmesan and float on top.

Serves 6

60 cloves of garlic (about 300 g/10 oz)

1.2 litres/2 pints **Brown Sauce Base**

150 ml/¼ pint milk

1.8 litres/3 pints water, plus extra to cover

salt and freshly ground black pepper

To garnish:
Parmesan cheese, grated

hot croûtons (optional)

Aubergines in Brandy Sauce

3 aubergines

50 g/2 oz butter

50 ml/2 fl oz groundnut oil

4 shallots, finely chopped

2 beefsteak tomatoes, skinned, deseeded and finely chopped

250 g/8 oz mushrooms, chopped

1 tablespoon chopped fresh thyme leaves

2 bay leaves

75 ml/3 fl oz brandy

150 ml/¼ pint Brown Sauce Base

salt and freshly ground black pepper

sprigs of thyme, to garnish

Alternatively:

CHICKEN IN BRANDY

Sauté 6 boned, seasoned chicken legs or breasts in oil and butter. Make the sauce and add the chicken at the same time as the thyme. Proceed as in the main recipe. To serve, fry 6 slices of bread in butter, place 1 slice on each plate, carve the chicken crossways, spoon the sauce on top and serve.

This sauce is not very plentiful, nor is it meant to be – but it is absolutely full of flavour, and delicious with aubergine – it's like ratatouille, but even more delicious! It is equally good with the boned chicken legs, as in the variation below.

Slice the aubergines lengthways, place in a single layer on a plate or tray, sprinkle with salt and set aside for 30 minutes to extract the bitter juices. Rinse with water and pat dry.

Heat the butter and two-thirds of the oil in a heavy-based pan, add the shallots and sauté until softened but not coloured. Add the chopped tomatoes and mushrooms. Cook until all the liquid has disappeared and the mixture started to brown, then add the thyme, bay leaves and brandy, bring to the boil and reduce until syrupy.

Add the Brown Sauce Base, cover and simmer slowly until the mixture dries out again – about 30 minutes: if not, raise the heat for 5 minutes or so until it does. Season to taste.

Brush a ridged, heavy-based frying pan with the remaining oil, and quickly char-grill the sliced aubergine. Turn the slices 45° and continue char-grilling until the surfaces are cross-hatched with grill marks. Repeat on the other side. Place 1 slice of aubergine on each heated dinner plate, pile the savoury mixture on top, then set a second slice of aubergine at right angles on top of the first. Serve with lambs' lettuce or similar peppery leaves, flakes of sea salt and cracked black pepper, and garnished with sprigs of thyme,

Serves 6

Tagliarini Verdi alla Pasticciata

3 eggs

1 large handful of cooked spinach, squeezed very dry

500 g/1 lb flour (type Italian 00)

For the meat sauce:
4 tablespoons olive oil

1 carrot, chopped

1 onion, chopped

1 celery stick, chopped

2 cloves garlic, crushed

a sprig of thyme

1 bay leaf

250 g/8 oz minced bacon

250 g/8 oz minced beef

150 ml/¼ pint white wine

3 tomatoes, skinned, deseeded and chopped

300 ml/½ pint Brown Sauce Base

50 g/2 oz chicken livers

For the white sauce:
25 g/1 oz butter

25 g/1 oz flour

300 ml/½ pint hot milk

6 tablespoons grated Parmesan cheese

salt and freshly ground black pepper

This should be made, as the name suggests, with fresh green spinach pasta. It was a much-loved speciality for many years at the old Speranza restaurant in Brompton Road, London – now long gone – and is one of the most delicious, as well as satisfying dishes in the old Italian manner.

In passing, I would mention that this green tagliarini also tastes delicious served plain with melted butter and grated Parmesan. Use a pasta machine if you have one, otherwise, follow the instructions below for making pasta by hand.

To make the tagliarini, blend the eggs and spinach in a liquidizer or food processor. Mix with the flour and knead into a ball. Roll out on a lightly floured work surface, roll up, and cut crossways into tagliarini.

To make the sauce, heat half the olive oil in a large non-stick pan, and fry the carrot, onion, celery and garlic until golden. Add the herbs, bacon and beef, stir well, and continue cooking until the meat browns. Add the white wine and tomatoes and cook until dry. Add the Brown Sauce Base, bring to the boil and simmer for about 40 minutes – the sauce should not be too thin or show too much oil. Remove and discard the thyme and bay leaf.

Heat the remaining oil in a small pan, and fry the chicken livers until browned, but still pink in the middle, then add them to the mixture. Taste and adjust the seasoning.

Boil the tagliarini in salted water until cooked (about 20 seconds) and drain well. Mix it into the meat sauce and divide the mixture between 6 round, flat, individual ovenproof dishes (or 1 large one). Set aside and keep warm.

Make a thick and creamy white sauce with the butter, flour and milk. Season with salt and freshly ground black pepper, and pour over the tagliarini, covering the pasta completely. Sprinkle the grated Parmesan over the top, brown under the grill and serve.

Serves 6

Soufflé of Sole Quenelles

This is one of those cooking miracles – you open the oven door and there is this incredible soufflé!

Don't be impatient and do it too soon. It will take time for the soufflé to rise and fill the bowl. More important still, don't let it rise on its first cooking or it won't rise on the second.

You could also substitute the Crab Bisque on page 102 for the fish fumet in this recipe.

To make the quenelles, melt the butter in a small saucepan. Stir in the flour and cook for 1 minute. Stir in the hot milk and cook, stirring, until the mixture has made a very thick white sauce. Season with salt and freshly ground black pepper and allow to cool.

Place the fillets of sole and 3 egg whites in a liquidizer or food processor and purée until smooth. Add the cooled sauce, pour the mixture into a bowl and season to taste. Whisk the remaining 3 egg whites to the soft peak stage and fold into the mixture.

Pour into 6 individual buttered ramekins and bake in a preheated oven at 140°C (275°F) Gas Mark 1 for 30 minutes, or until set. Cool a little. Turn out and wrap in clingfilm, or use immediately.

To make the sauce, melt the butter in a small frying pan, add the shallots and simmer for a few minutes. Add the white wine, bring to the boil and reduce until syrupy. Add the fish stock, then the Brown Sauce Base, the chopped shellfish shells and tomato purée, mix well and simmer for 20 minutes.

In another pan, mix the flour with the lobster butter or butter and strain the hot sauce into the pan. Whisk in the cream, tarragon and lots of pepper. Bring to the boil, stirring, and cook until the mixture reaches a soupy consistency. You should have about 900 ml/1½ pints.

To assemble, divide the sauce between 6 deep, ovenproof soup bowls or individual casseroles, then slip in the quenelles, and cook in a preheated oven at 240°C (475°F) Gas Mark 9.

When fully souffléed (about 20 minutes, or up to 40 minutes, if you've chilled them earlier), place the bowls on underplates and serve.

Serves 6

50–65 g/2–2½ oz butter

3 tablespoons flour

150 ml/¼ pint hot milk

250 g/8 oz fillets of sole

6 egg whites

For the sauce
(makes 900 ml/1½ pints):
25 g/1 oz butter

2 shallots, chopped

300 ml/½ pint white wine

450 ml/¾ pint fish stock
or shellfish fumet

300 ml/½ pint
Brown Sauce Base

a couple of handfuls of
shellfish; crab, lobster, prawns,
including the shells

1 teaspoon tomato purée

1 tablespoon flour

75 g/3 oz lobster butter
(see method on page 108),
or butter

150 ml/¼ pint whipping cream

1 tablespoon chopped,
fresh tarragon leaves

salt and lots of freshly
ground black pepper

Lobster Américaine

1 live lobster

50 g/2 oz unsalted butter

50 ml/2 fl oz olive oil

2 tablespoons brandy

75 ml/3 fl oz white wine

125 ml/4 fl oz fish stock

150 ml/¼ pint
Brown Sauce Base

a sprig of thyme

a bay leaf

parsley stalks

1 tablespoon chopped tarragon

salt and pepper

sprigs of watercress or tarragon

fleurons of pastry

Alternatively:

PASTRY SHELLS

Brush 12 scallop shells with oil. Cover the outside of 6 shells with puff pastry, tucking it over the edge. Place another shell on top, to sandwich the pastry between. Cook in a preheated oven at 220°C (425°F) Gas Mark 7 for 15 minutes. Trim the excess pastry from around the scallop shells and pull the shells apart. Spectacular, but easy!

This dish needs a raw lobster, alive and kicking, but it can be made with one that has been 'chilled to sleep' for a few minutes in the freezer. This retains all the juices essential for the sauce – and it is as humane a way of dispatching it as any.

Split the lobster in half and clean it, keeping any of the liver and roe to make the lobster butter. Break off the lobster's claws, and reserve.

To make the lobster butter, blend the roe, the liver and butter until smooth, then chill.

Heat the olive oil in a large pan, and fry the claws and the lobster, shell-side down. When the lobster has turned a very bright red, remove the pan from the heat, carefully pour the brandy over and ignite, shaking the pan well until the flames die down.

Remove all the pieces from the pan and set aside. Add the white wine, bring to the boil, and reduce to a syrup. Add the fish stock, the Brown Sauce Base, the thyme, bay leaf and parsley stalks, a good grinding of pepper and some salt.

Bring to the boil, return the lobster to the pan, reduce the heat, cover and simmer for 5 minutes. Remove the lobster, take the meat carefully from the tail and keep warm. Chop up the shell and return it to the pan for a further 25 minutes. After 15 minutes, take out the claws, remove their meat and add to the tail meat.

Strain the sauce into a clean pan. Rinse the shell pieces in a small bowl of clean water, then add the water to the sauce.

Bring the sauce to the boil and reduce it to about 250 ml/8 fl oz. Taste, and adjust the seasoning. Add the tarragon to the sauce, and beat in the butter or lobster butter (if using).

To serve, pour the sauce on to 2 heated dinner plates, arrange the lobster tail and the claws on top, and garnish with sprigs of watercress or tarragon and the fleurons. Alternatively, substitute Pastry Shells (recipe left) for the fleurons and set at an angle, as in the photograph. *Serves 2*

Brandied Tarragon Chicken

1 tablespoon groundnut oil

1 large capon, or roasting chicken, about 1–1.5 kg/2–3 lb, cut into 6 portions

300 ml/½ pint white wine

50 ml/2 fl oz brandy

1 clove garlic, sliced

900 ml/1½ pints Brown Sauce Base

3 sprigs of tarragon

1 teaspoon green peppercorns (optional)

150 ml/¼ pint chicken stock

salt and freshly ground black pepper

Alternatively:

JUNIPER PORK WITH TARRAGON AND ROSEMARY

Substitute 6 large, trimmed, pork neck cutlets for the chicken, and add 1 large sprig of rosemary and 10 juniper berries, crushed with 1 teaspoon of salt. Use chicken or veal stock and proceed as in the main recipe, but increasing the cooking time to 40 minutes.

'Chicken in Tarragon' seems to be inextricably linked in most people's minds with a traditional creamy sauce. So – just to be perverse – here is a fragrant brown alternative.

This recipe is equally delicious with pork. Prepare it exactly as the main recipe, but add extra flavourings in the form of rosemary and juniper berries and cook a little longer to make sure the pork is cooked thoroughly. Suitable accompaniments are vegetables such as Creamed Celeriac (see page 114), good mashed potatoes, and perhaps spinach, fried in a little butter then sprinkled with toasted sesame seeds, either plain, or pounded in a mortar.

Heat the oil in a non-stick pan, and fry the capon pieces, turning them frequently, until evenly browned all over.

Pour off the excess fat, season with salt and freshly ground black pepper, and place the pieces in a casserole dish.

Add the wine, brandy and garlic to the pan, bring to the boil, and reduce to 2 tablespoons. Add the Brown Sauce Base, sprigs of tarragon and green peppercorns, if using. Season well and add the stock.

Pour the liquid over the chicken in the casserole dish, and cover. Place in a preheated oven at 180°C (350°F) Gas Mark 4 for about 20–25 minutes until the chicken is cooked through.

Transfer the chicken pieces into a deep serving dish. Remove any excess fat from the casserole, then boil the sauce until it reaches a coating consistency. Taste, and adjust the seasoning, pour the sauce over the chicken and serve with Lyonnaise potatoes and a salad.

Serves 6

Chicken Bordelaise

A Bordelaise Sauce includes onions, white wine and parsley. Cook these together with a little oil and butter plus the Brown Sauce Base, and you have a mixture that will transform any dish into a delicious occasion. As a variation, try adding the cèpes and the garlic to the potatoes instead of the chicken – it makes a nice change. Dried cèpes are also imported from Italy, where they are known as 'porcini'.

Cut the chicken breasts in half again, leaving them on the bone. (Use the wing tips and backbone, with carrot and onion, to make a stock for another occasion.)

Heat the oil and butter in a pan and brown the chicken joints. Add the onion, and cook gently until softened but not coloured, covering the pan for 5 minutes. Remove the pieces of chicken to a plate, and set aside in a warm place.

Add the wine and garlic to the pan, and bring to the boil. Reduce until syrupy, then add the Brown Sauce Base, and boil for 2 minutes more. Replace the chicken and add the thyme and the bay leaf. Add the sliced, reconstituted cèpes or porcini (if using), together with the strained steeping liquid, to the pan, then cover and simmer until the chicken is cooked through. Sprinkle over the fresh parsley, and cook for a further 2 minutes.

Transfer the chicken joints on to a serving plate and keep warm. Bring the sauce to the boil and reduce a little if necessary, then spoon over the chicken.

Meanwhile, heat the oil and butter in a pan, and fry the onion slices gently until softened but not coloured. Add the potatoes and cook for 3–4 minutes. Add the chicken stock and seasoning, bring to the boil, cover, and simmer to finish cooking the potatoes. When they are nearly done, remove the lid so that the liquid will evaporate and the potatoes dry out. Spoon them around the chicken, and serve.

Serves 6

1 roasting chicken, about
2.5 kg/5 lb, cut into joints

1 tablespoon groundnut oil

50 g/2 oz butter

1 large onion
(not Spanish), sliced

300 ml/½ pint white wine

2 cloves of garlic, crushed

450 ml/¾ pint
Brown Sauce Base

a sprig of thyme

1 bay leaf

2–3 dried cèpes or porcini,
reconstituted for 30 minutes
in 1 cup of boiling water (optional)

salt and freshly
ground black pepper

2 tablespoons chopped, fresh,
flat leaf parsley, to garnish

For the potatoes:
25 ml/1 fl oz groundnut oil

50 g/2 oz butter

1 large onion, sliced

1.25 kg/2½ lb firm
potatoes, sliced

300 ml/½ pint
light chicken stock

salt and freshly
ground black pepper

Coq au Vin

1 large capon or roasting chicken, about 2.5 kg/5 lb

1 tablespoon chopped fresh thyme leaves, or 1 teaspoon dried

25 ml/1 fl oz groundnut oil

50 ml/2 fl oz brandy

1 bottle of red wine

900 ml/1½ pints Brown Sauce Base

salt and freshly ground black pepper

To garnish:
12 shallots, peeled but left whole

150 ml/¼ pint red wine vinegar

1 tablespoon sugar

125 g/4 oz unsalted butter

175 g/6 oz baby mushrooms

lemon juice, to taste

375 g/12 oz green bacon, cut into 2.5 cm/1 inch cubes

Note:

SLAKED CORNFLOUR
It has become unfashionable, since the advent of *Nouvelle Cuisine*, to use cornflour as a thickener. This I believe is a mistake. It certainly isn't fattening, and is traditional in dishes such as Oxtail. Why waste good sauce?

Often this dish is made with a specified wine, when it becomes 'Coq au Chambertin' or whatever. Although, technically speaking, the wine is usually a red, a dry white wine is equally suitable. Try it for a change, adding a sprig of tarragon (see Brandied Tarragon Chicken on page 110). You will be pleasantly surprised!

Start to prepare the garnish first. Simmer the shallots in salted water for 10 minutes, then drain. Pour the vinegar into a small saucepan, add the sugar and 75 g/3 oz of the butter, and boil until syrupy. Add the shallots and simmer for 5 minutes. Set aside to macerate, but pour off the syrup before adding the shallots to the final dish.

Joint the chicken, cut each joint into 2, and roll them in the thyme. Heat the oil in a large pan, and fry the chicken pieces, skin-side down, until very brown. Don't attempt to brown the flesh – just the skin (flesh dries out and becomes inedible when it browns).

Remove the pan from the heat, pour over the brandy and ignite, shaking the pan to spread the flames. Remove the chicken from the pan and set aside. Pour in the red wine, bring to the boil and reduce until thick and syrupy.

Add the Brown Sauce Base, taste and adjust the seasoning. Return the chicken joints to the sauce, cover and simmer for 40 minutes.

Lift the chicken into a large bowl, bring the sauce to the boil and reduce to about 900 ml/1½ pints. If it is still too thin, thicken it with a little cornflour slaked in water. Taste, adjust the seasoning, then return the chicken to the sauce.

To prepare the rest of the garnish, melt the remaining butter in a small pan, and sauté the baby mushrooms until lightly browned, then add a very little lemon juice.

Place the cubed bacon in a small saucepan, with water to cover, bring to the boil, and simmer until tender. Change the water once if the bacon is salty.

Add the mushrooms, shallots and bacon to the chicken and sauce, simmer for 5 minutes, then serve with boiled new potatoes, such as the pretty and delicious pink fir apples.

Serves 6

Duck with Salsify and Port

My first choice for this dish would be Barbary duck. It has far less blubber under the skin, and the meat is lean and full of flavour. Gressingham is a close second, but can be hard to find. Aylesbury ducks were legendary as the best breed in Britain but, alas, those days are long gone, and I find the modern breed of Aylesbury a great disappointment – nowhere near as good as it used to be.

When preparing the salsify, or its cousin the scorzanera, it is important not to break them, or nick the skin or, like beetroot, they will 'bleed' into the water and their delicate flavour lost.

Potato pancakes would make a delicious accompaniment – just wonderful for mopping up all the juices and the sauce.

To prepare the salsify or scorzanera, carefully rinse off any clinging dirt and simmer whole in a long pan or small fish kettle. When cooked, but still *al dente*, refresh under cold running water and pinch off the black skin. Cut into 3.5 cm/1½ inch pieces and set aside.

To prepare the ducks, prick them all over and rub with salt. Place in a roasting tin, back-to-back, and cook in a preheated oven at 200°C (400°F) Gas Mark 6 for 40 minutes. Turn the ducks breast-to-breast and continue cooking for 30 minutes. Turn them on their backs, reduce the temperature to 180°C (350°F) Gas Mark 4 and cook for another 20 minutes. Test by piercing with a skewer in the thickest part of a thigh. The ducks are cooked if the juices run clear. If still pink, continue cooking until done. Remove and keep warm.

Pour off the excess fat from the pan and deglaze it with the port. Bring to the boil and reduce until the flavour is concentrated. Add the Brown Sauce Base, stock and lots of freshly ground black pepper. Bring to the boil and check the thickness of the sauce – and boil down a little more if not thick enough. Taste and adjust the seasoning, then add the pieces of salsify or scorzanera to warm through.

Carve the duck and serve with the port sauce and salsify.

Serves 6

3 long sticks salsify or scorzanera

2 ducks, preferably Barbary or Gressingham

150 ml/¼ pint ruby port

300 ml/½ pint Brown Sauce Base

150 ml/¼ pint stock

salt and freshly ground black pepper

Note:

SALSIFY AND SCORZANERA

Salsify, or oyster plant, is now becoming more widely available. The ones you see in shops are almost always its cousin, the black-skinned scorzanera, which is easier to peel and tastes virtually identical. It is also delicious served by itself as a first course, with a simple Hollandaise dressing (see page 19), and this way its flavour is more easily appreciated.

Barbary Duck Breasts with Apples and Creamed Celeriac

3 large Barbary duck breasts, or 6 magrets

1 tablespoon lemon juice

salt and freshly ground black pepper

For the Burgundy sauce:
25 g/1 oz butter

3 shallots, chopped

25 ml/1 fl oz brandy

300 ml/½ pint red Burgundy

450 ml/¾ pint Brown Sauce Base

For the creamed celeriac:
Cream Sauce Base (see page 52), made with 150 ml/¼ pint whipping cream

1 celeriac, peeled

To garnish:
1 tablespoon butter

125 g/4 oz button mushrooms

½ teaspoon lemon juice

2 red apples, cored and sliced, but not peeled

18 Glazed Onions (see page 164)

The celeriac goes so well with duck breasts in this dish that it becomes a 'must'; but it should be said that celeriac done like this is delicious with many other meats.

To prepare the garnish, melt the butter in a small frying pan and sauté the button mushrooms until browned. Sprinkle with the lemon juice. Remove and set aside. Add the apple slices to the pan, fry until nicely golden, and set aside. Cook the Glazed Onions (see page 164). Keep all the garnishes warm until ready to serve.

To make the Burgundy Sauce, melt the butter in a pan and cook the shallots until softened but not coloured. Add the brandy and the wine, bring to the boil and reduce until syrupy. Add the Brown Sauce Base, bring back to the boil, simmer for at least 10 minutes, then strain. Taste and adjust the seasoning. Add a little stock or water to thin out, if necessary.

To prepare the duck breasts, trim off the excess fat, prick the skin all over, and season on both sides. Heat a non-stick pan until very hot, and fry the breasts, skin side down, until well browned. Pour off the duck fat, turn the breasts over and rest them in a warm place.

Return the Burgundy sauce to the boil, pour into an ovenproof dish, and place the duck breasts on top. Cook in a preheated oven at 150°C (300°F) Gas Mark 2 for about 10 minutes to heat the sauce through and amalgamate the juices.

To make the Creamed Celeriac, boil the whipping cream to a thick, mayonnaise-like consistency, as in Step 3, page 52. Season with black pepper and salt. Grate the peeled celeriac, add to the cream and heat through quickly. Check seasoning and serve as soon as possible.

Remove the duck breasts from the sauce, place them on a board, cut lengthways into slices 1 cm/½ inch thick, and spread the slices into a fan shape. Spoon the celeriac on to heated dinner plates, and place the fans of duck breast over the top. Spoon the Burgundy sauce beside the duck, and add the garnish of fried red apple slices, the Glazed Onions and the lemon-flavoured button mushrooms.

Serves 6

Roast Duck with Port and Peppercorn Sauce

3 small Gressingham ducks

150 ml/¼ pint port

25 ml/1 fl oz brandy

25 g/1 oz green peppercorns

**300 ml/½ pint
Brown Sauce Base**

300 ml/½ pint chicken stock

1 teaspoon cornflour

**salt and freshly
ground black pepper**

Accompaniment:
OLIVE MASH

When a sauce is rich, with strong flavours, such as this one with port and peppercorns, I like to serve a vegetable which has an assertive but not overwhelming taste. It should also be good for mopping-up purposes – you don't want to waste all that terrific sauce. I suggest an olive mash of potato with celeriac or parsnip (using half-and-half olive oil and butter to make the mash).

Why do port and peppercorns go so well together? There was a time when green peppercorns were new and all the rage and therefore added to everything. They are certainly more pleasant to eat than crunching on black ones, and then having to drink pints of water to alleviate the symptoms. Nowadays, combined with duck, they hold a permanent place in the cookery books.

Rub the ducks all over with salt, place in a roasting tin, back to back, and cook in a preheated oven at 200°C (400°F) Gas Mark 6 for about 40 minutes. Turn the ducks breast-to-breast and continue cooking for 30 minutes. Turn them on their backs, reduce the temperature to 180°C (350°F) Gas Mark 4 and cook for another 20 minutes. Test by piercing with a skewer in the thickest part of a thigh. The ducks are cooked if the juices run clear. If still pink, continue cooking until done. Remove the ducks from the oven and cut off the breasts and legs; keep warm. Chop up the carcasses.

Pour off as much fat as possible from the roasting tin, add the port, brandy and peppercorns to the pan, bring to the boil and reduce until nearly all the liquid has disappeared. Crush the peppercorns with a fork and return the carcasses to the roasting tin. Cover with the Brown Sauce Base and stock, and bring to the boil. Simmer for 10 minutes, strain into a clean pan and reduce the sauce if necessary until it reaches a pouring consistency. Taste, and adjust the seasoning. Add a little cornflour dissolved in water if there is still too much fat from the duck floating on the top, and thin out with water if necessary.

To serve, place the duck on heated dinner plates, and pour the sauce beside. Serve with an Olive Mash of potato and celeriac or potato and parsnip (see note, left).

Serves 6

Duck Breasts in Orange Burgundy Sauce

If you make the sauce in advance, it will take about 20 minutes to finish the dish, of which only 15 minutes is cooking time.

Serve this dish garnished with the Brandied Kumquats on page 170 – an amazingly versatile recipe which I have also used as an accompaniment to the sinful pudding recipe on page 185 – White Chocolate Mousse with Three Chocolate Sauces.

If using the optional brandied kumquat garnish, prepare them first and set aside in a warm place.

To prepare the orange Burgundy sauce, heat the butter in a frying pan, add the onion and cook until softened but not coloured. Add the brandy and cook for a further 2 minutes. Add the red wine, bring to the boil and reduce to a syrup. Add the Brown Sauce Base and the peppercorns, and simmer for about 40 minutes, adding water if it becomes too thick. Strain the sauce, taste, and adjust the seasoning, then set aside and keep warm.

Trim any excess fat from the duck breasts, prick the skin all over and season on both sides.

Heat a non-stick pan until very hot. Add the breasts, skin-side down, and brown them well, pressing the fat out of the skin. Pour off the fat from time to time to keep the meat 'dry', but reserve it for another use, such as frying potatoes. Turn the breasts over in the pan and set them aside in a warm place to rest and finish cooking.

Return the sauce to the boil, then add the redcurrant jelly, stirring until dissolved. Add the duck juices and orange zest.

Slice the duck breasts lengthways into a fan shape, arrange on 6 individual serving plates. Pour the sauce around, garnish with the Brandied Kumquats, if using, and serve.

Serves 6

3 large duck breasts, or 6 magrets

salt and freshly ground black pepper

For the orange Burgundy sauce:
25 g/1 oz butter

1 onion, chopped

150 ml/¼ pint brandy

300 ml/½ pint red Burgundy, or other deep red wine

900 ml /1½ pints Brown Sauce Base

10 whole black peppercorns, crushed

2 teaspoons good redcurrant jelly

zest of 1 orange

Brandied Kumquats (see page 170), to garnish (optional)

Duck Hams in Green Olives

12 duck legs

175 ml/6 fl oz brandy

2 tomatoes, skinned, deseeded and finely chopped

24 green olives, pitted and chopped

1 sprig of thyme

1 sprig of rosemary

1 bay leaf

2 cloves garlic, crushed

50 g/2 oz butter

3 shallots, chopped

300 ml/½ pint white wine

350 ml/12 fl oz Brown Sauce Base

salt and pepper

Alternatively:

CONFIT OF DUCK

Cover 6 duck legs with sea salt and chill for 24 hours. Rinse, pat dry, place in a deep pan and pour in melted duck fat to cover. Cook slowly, with the fat barely simmering, for 40 minutes. Remove the duck from the pan to a glazed earthenware pot and pour over the fat until completely covered. Store for 6 months in a cool place.

A very useful and delicious way of using leftover legs of duck, although many butchers now sell the legs separately, as well as the breasts. If using whole ducks, you can use the breasts for recipes such as those on pages 83, 114 or 117, and the carcasses as stock for recipes such as Veal Escalopes with Creamy Mushrooms on page 138.

Reserve the duck fat (it can be kept in the refrigerator) and use to roast or sauté all kinds of meats and vegetables: it is especially good with potatoes. It can also be used to make confits of duck.

A confit is a traditional French farmhouse method of preserving duck or goose. It can be bought in tins, but is interesting to make yourself. When cooking duck or goose, reserve the fat and when you have 500 g–1 kg/1–2 lb, try the recipe below. The rather salty flavour is typical. To use, add to your Cassoulet (page 146) or heat the confit in its fat, then remove the meat to a serving dish. Cook sliced potatoes in the fat and serve with the meat, sprinkled with chopped, fresh, flat leaf parsley.

Prick the duck legs all over with a skewer or small, sharp knife.

Heat a non-stick pan, and brown the duck legs. Pour off excess fat, and reserve for another use. Warm half the brandy in a ladle, pour over the duck, ignite and shake the pan until the flames die down. Remove the duck legs and keep warm. Add the rest of the brandy to the pan, the tomatoes, olives, thyme, rosemary, bay leaf and garlic, bring to the boil and reduce until thickened, then add the duck legs. Taste, and adjust the seasoning, cover and simmer for 45 minutes.

Meanwhile, heat the butter in a small pan, and sauté the shallots for about 5 minutes. Add the white wine, bring to the boil and reduce until syrupy. Add the Brown Sauce Base and simmer for 40 minutes more. Taste and adjust the seasoning, then strain over the cooked duck legs. Continue to simmer for another 5–10 minutes so that the flavours mingle. I like to serve them with triangles of golden fried bread, but boiled noodles would also be a suitable accompaniment. *Serves 6*

Casserole of Turkey Drumsticks

This is a recipe where, having made the sauce base, you really reap the reward. The technique is the same for any meat – the flavour, of course, varies with the choice of meat. You need little more than five minutes to put this dish together.

Heat the oil in a frying pan, and brown the turkey legs evenly all over. Pour off excess fat and dust the turkey with paprika, to taste.

Add the Brown Sauce Base, water, freshly ground black pepper, and salt to taste. Bring to the boil, reduce the heat, cover and simmer the turkey until tender, about 45 minutes to 1½ hours, depending on size.

Remove and discard the bones, and place the meat on a serving dish. Correct the sauce consistency, reducing further if necessary. Taste and adjust the seasoning.

Pour the sauce over the meat and serve with tiny steamed vegetables or sautéed chestnut mushrooms.

Serves 6

1 tablespoon groundnut oil

2 large (or 4 small) turkey legs

1–3 teaspoons paprika, to taste

300 ml/½ pint **Brown Sauce Base**

300 ml/½ pint water

salt and freshly ground black pepper

Garlic Roast Haunch of Turkey

Many new cuts of turkey are now available. Roast these turkey thighs as if they were small legs of lamb – with garlic and rosemary. Wrap them in smoked bacon to add flavour.

Wrap the turkey thighs in smoked bacon, securing with toothpicks if necessary. Place in a lightly oiled roasting tin, and tuck the rosemary sprigs and garlic cloves underneath. Roast in a preheated oven at 200°C (400°F) Gas Mark 6 until a skewer inserted into the thickest part of the meat comes out clean. Remove the meat and keep warm.

Pour off all but 2 tablespoons of the pan juices, add the white wine and reduce until syrupy. Add the Brown Sauce Base and stir. Add a little water or stock if the gravy is too thick.

Remove the toothpicks, carve the turkey lengthways, parallel to the bone, and serve with the gravy, crispy bacon and roast potatoes.

Serves 6

2 turkey thighs

6 rashers smoked bacon

2 sprigs of rosemary

6 cloves garlic, crushed

150 ml/¼ pint white wine

300 ml/½ pint **Brown Sauce Base**

a little chicken stock or water, (see method)

Roast Quail with a Tea-scented Sauce

This is a delicious, elegant recipe for quail. The bones can be fiddly to deal with on the plate, so it's better to do most of the bone removal before serving. However, to conserve the delicate, elusive flavour of this meat, it is important to cook the meat on the bone.

To prepare the pretty, toasted hearts in the photograph, follow the variation below right.

To make the sauce, first soak the raisins in the tea for at least 1 hour or overnight, until required.

Heat two-thirds of the butter in a saucepan, add the shallots, bay leaf and cloves, and cook gently until the shallots are softened but not coloured. Add the wine, bring to the boil and reduce gently until syrupy. Pour in the Brown Sauce Base, simmer for 10 minutes, then transfer into a roasting tin.

Place the slices of bread on a baking tray.

Heat the groundnut oil in a heavy non-stick frying pan. When very hot, add the quail and brown them on all sides; the breasts should have a good colour. Lay the birds side by side in the roasting tin and place in a preheated oven at 240°C (475°F) Gas Mark 9, for 5 minutes. Place the tray of buttered bread in the oven to crisp; remove when toasted and golden.

Cut the breast from each bird, season with salt and freshly ground black pepper and keep warm. Remove the legs, chop up the carcasses, return these to the tin and place back in the oven to simmer for about 5 minutes.

Return the legs, breasts and oven-fried bread to the oven to reheat for a few minutes.

Meanwhile, strain the sauce into a pan, add the tea and raisins, bring to the boil, reduce to a light coating consistency, then beat in the remaining butter to finish the sauce.

Divide the toast between heated plates and arrange the legs and breasts on top. Spoon the sauce beside and garnish with sprigs of a suitable herb, such as winter savoury or bay leaves.

Serves 6

6–12 slices white bread, buttered well on one side

1 tablespoon groundnut oil

12 quail

salt and freshly ground black pepper

For the tea-scented sauce:
75 g/3 oz raisins

300 ml/½ pint strong, hot, Earl Grey tea

75 g/3 oz butter

2 shallots, chopped

1 bay leaf

3 cloves

300 ml/½ pint dry Riesling

450 ml/¾ pint Brown Sauce Base

sprigs of winter savoury or bay leaves, to garnish

Alternatively:

GOLDEN, CRISPY TOAST HEARTS

Cut out heart shapes from the slices of bread, butter well on one side and toast in the oven as in the main recipe.

Braised Guinea Fowl with Bacon and Puy Lentils

175 g/6 oz Puy lentils

butter for frying

250 g/8 oz bacon, cubed

1 onion, chopped

3 carrots, sliced

2 guinea fowl, jointed

25 ml/1 fl oz Calvados

300 ml/½ pint white wine

300 ml/½ pint
Brown Sauce Base

1 tablespoon chopped
fresh thyme leaves

150 ml/¼ pint water

salt and freshly
ground black pepper

To garnish:
25 g/1 oz butter

125 g/4 oz breadcrumbs

2 tablespoons chopped
fresh, flat leaf parsley

Guinea fowl are not as gamey as pheasant, but they certainly have a fuller flavour than the average chicken, and unless you obtain a young Cornish hen – usually called a 'gleaney' (presumably from the Latin 'galina', meaning 'hen'), they do need a longer cooking time.

When I first cooked this recipe, I used red lentils, but now there are many more varieties available, including these beautiful green 'lentilles de Puy', from France.

Wash the lentils, place them in a saucepan, cover with water, bring to the boil and simmer gently until tender. Drain off any excess liquid.

Heat the butter in a large pan and add the bacon pieces, onion and sliced carrots. Add the pieces of guinea fowl and fry them, skin-side down, until browned. Pour over the Calvados and set alight with a match, shaking the pan to spread the flames. When the flames have died down, remove the guinea fowl and set aside, add the wine, bring to the boil and reduce until syrupy.

Add the Brown Sauce Base, thyme leaves and the measured water and bring to the boil. Add the leg pieces of the birds, simmer for about 20 minutes then add the breast sections and simmer for 20 minutes more, thus preventing the 'white' meat from overcooking.

Meanwhile, prepare the garnish. Heat the butter in a small pan, add the breadcrumbs and fry until nicely browned. Stir in the parsley.

Lift all the meat on to a heated serving dish, then bring the sauce remaining in the pan to the boil and reduce by half. Add the lentils, simmer for 5 minutes until the mixture is nicely moist – neither too dry nor too sloppy. Taste and adjust the seasoning.

Spoon the mixture onto the serving dish, in a ring around the guinea fowl. Sprinkle with the fried breadcrumbs and parsley.

Serves 6

Fillet of Beef with a Red Wine and Mushroom Sauce

Since there is so little work to do preparing the meat, you will have time to concentrate on the sauce. Many varieties of wild mushrooms are now available in Britain but if you can find only very delicate oyster mushrooms, which haven't a lot of taste, you should add a few soaked dried cèpes or morels to pep up the sauce.

If you are using dried mushrooms first steep them in 300 ml/½ pint water, preferably overnight (otherwise pour boiling water over them and leave for 10 minutes). Strain the mushrooms then strain the steeping water into a bowl through muslin or a coffee filter paper, and reserve the water. If using morels, carefully rinse them free of dirt in several changes of water.

If using soaked dried mushrooms, simmer them and the oyster mushrooms in the steeping water for 5 minutes with 50 g/2 oz of the butter and the chopped chives. Otherwise use fresh wild mushrooms, and simmer them in plain water.

In a separate pan, heat a further 50 g/2 oz butter, add the shallots and garlic and cook until softened but not coloured. Add the wine, bring to the boil, then simmer until syrupy. Add the Brown Sauce Base, simmer for 10 minutes, strain and add to the mushroom liquor.

Season the tournedos, then heat the remaining butter in a hot pan and fry the meat to your liking. Remove and keep warm in a low oven.

Pour the sauce into the pan, bring to the boil and reduce to a light coating consistency.

To prepare the garnish of fresh oyster mushrooms, melt the butter in a small pan, add the mushrooms and sauté them briefly. Season with salt and freshly ground black pepper.

To prepare the tomato cubes, warm them briefly in another small pan, and season as before.

Place the steaks on heated dinner plates, pour the sauce around and garnish with the sautéed oyster mushrooms and the warmed tomato cubes.

Serves 6

25 g/1 oz dried cèpes (porcini) or morels, or 50 g/2 oz fresh wild mushrooms, cut into chunks

175 g/6 oz butter

1 tablespoon chopped fresh chives

3 shallots, chopped

2 garlic cloves, crushed

150 ml/¼ pint red wine

300 ml/½ pint Brown Sauce Base

6 tournedos or steaks, about 175 g/6 oz each

salt and freshly ground black pepper

To garnish:
25 g/1 oz butter

250 g/8 oz yellow oyster mushrooms

1 tomato, skinned, deseeded and diced

Char-grilled Steak with Fresh Horseradish and Devilled Sauces

The perfect dish for people who like their food hot and spicy. You will need only a crusty loaf of bread with it, and perhaps some deep-fried celery tops. Use the finest grater blade of the food processor to grate the horseradish. Cook these steaks by dry-frying on a ridged pan – a griddle – or in a non-stick frying pan, or in an ordinary pan with a little olive oil.

These same sauces are terrific with char-grilled swordfish or tuna, a fish which is often teamed with spicy sauces in American and Mediterranean cooking (see below right). Serve the fish with grilled or roasted vegetables such as the Pickled Peppers on page 131, and a leafy green salad.

Lightly oil a griddle or frying pan and heat until very hot. Season the steaks, and cook as you like; rare, medium or well-done. Keep warm.

Place the grated horseradish in a bowl. Add the vinegar, cream and a little salt. Whisk until thick and fluffy and use within 1 hour.

To make the devilled sauce, melt half the butter in a pan, add the shallots, vinegar, wine and peppercorns, bring to the boil and reduce until syrupy. Add the Brown Sauce Base and stock, bring to the boil and simmer for 20 minutes until reduced to a coating consistency.

Beat in the rest of the butter, the Worcestershire sauce and the salt.

Place one steak on each heated dinner plate, place a large spoonful of horse-radish on top, and pour the devilled sauce beside.

Serves 6

6 steaks, fillet or rump

salt and freshly ground black pepper

For the horseradish sauce:
1 tablespoon finely grated fresh horseradish

2 teaspoons white wine vinegar

150 ml/¼ pint double cream

salt

For the devilled sauce (poivrade):
50 g/2 oz butter

3 shallots, chopped

125 ml/4 fl oz red wine vinegar

175 g/6 fl oz red wine

1 teaspoon coarsely ground black peppercorns

300 ml/½ pint Brown Sauce Base

150 ml/¼ pint beef stock

1 teaspoon Worcestershire Sauce

salt

Alternatively:
TUNA WITH TWO HOT SAUCES
Char-grill 6 seasoned tuna steaks and proceed as in the main recipe, substituting fish stock for beef stock.

Provençal Beef Daube

1 tablespoon olive oil

1.25 kg/2½ lb lean
beef rib, boned and rolled

3 sprigs of thyme

3 cloves of garlic, sliced

1 bay leaf

1 large onion, chopped

150 ml/¼ pint white wine

150 ml/¼ pint beef stock

300 ml/½ pint
Brown Sauce Base

12 black and green olives, pitted

salt and freshly
ground black pepper

A daube needs a long cooking time, and a pot just big enough to hold the meat in one piece. If you like very lean meat, use topside instead of boned and rolled beef, but it will not have the same succulence.

Heat the oil in a large pan and brown the meat on both sides. Season and transfer to an ovenproof casserole. Add the thyme, garlic, bay leaf and onion to the pan and cook gently until softened but not coloured. Add the wine, bring to the boil and reduce by half. Add the stock, bring to the boil and pour into the casserole.

Cook, covered, in a preheated oven at 120°C (250°F) Gas Mark ½, for about 2–3 hours, by which time the meat should have absorbed nearly all the juices and the edges should be beginning to brown. Pour off the fat without losing any of the browned flavouring bits.

Bring the Brown Sauce Base to the boil in a separate pan, add the olives and a little water to thin it. Pour it over the meat and gently mix with the juices. Disturb the meat as little as possible, as it is now very tender and will break up easily.

Return the casserole to the oven for a further 30 minutes, then serve the daube with creamy mashed potatoes.

Serves 6

Boeuf Bourguignon

1 tablespoon olive oil

1.5 kg/3 lb feather steak,
cut in 3.5 cm/1½ inch cubes

50 ml/2 fl oz brandy

¾ bottle red Burgundy

600 ml/1 pint
Brown Sauce Base

1 sprig of thyme

salt and freshly
ground black pepper

One of the great classics of French bourgeois cooking – very easy and delicious when made with Brown Sauce Base. Use a medium quality wine if possible, and one that is not too acid.

Heat the oil in a heavy-based casserole and brown the meat. Pour in the brandy, ignite and shake the pan to spread the flames. Remove the meat, add the wine and reduce until syrupy (about 2 tablespoons).

Mix well, add the Brown Sauce Base, thyme, a little salt and lots of pepper. Return the meat to the casserole, bring to the boil, cover and simmer in the oven at 150°C (300°F) Gas Mark 2 for about 2 hours.

Remove from the oven and reduce the sauce, or thicken with a little slaked arrowroot. Serve with lots of mashed potatoes and a leafy salad.

Serves 6

Braised Beef with Pistou

When you read through this recipe you will realise that the meat never actually boils or fries. The result is a unique texture which is comparable only with British savoury puddings cooked in a suet crust. It makes a delicious hot summer dish, scented with herbs and sprinkled with Parmesan – all the flavours of Italy!

This method of marinating meat is very easy and effective. With large joints of meat such as the Roast Saddle of Hare in a Creamy Sauce on page 91, you can knead the marinade into the meat while it's inside the plastic bag – a method that, once you've tried it, you will want to use in other recipes.

Place the garlic, thyme, olives and olive oil in a large plastic bag stretched over a bowl. Season the meat with salt and freshly ground black pepper, and place it in the bag. Remove from the bowl, squash out the air, knot the bag then knead to mix the oil and seasonings with the beef. Leave in the refrigerator for 2 hours or overnight.

Pour the Brown Sauce Base into a saucepan, bring it to the boil, pour it into a slow cooker or heavy casserole dish, then add the meat and the remaining contents of the plastic bag. Stir well and cook in a preheated oven at 120°C (250°F) Gas Mark ½, or at 120°C in the slow cooker for 3 hours.

Pour off the liquid into a saucepan, bring to the boil and reduce to a light coating consistency. Stir in the basil, and season to taste.

Pour 1.8 litres/3 pints of water into a large saucepan, add the salt and olive oil, and bring to the boil. Add the tagliarini and cook for about 4–6 minutes or until it rises to the surface of the boiling water. Drain the pasta and stir in the butter.

Place the beef on heated dinner plates, and serve accompanied by the tagliarini, sprinkled with the Parmesan.

Serves 6

6 cloves of garlic, crushed

2 sprigs thyme

18 black olives, pitted

50 ml/2 fl oz olive oil

1.5 kg/3 lb flank or similar stewing beef, cut into 2.5 cm/1 inch cubes

600 ml/1 pint Brown Sauce Base

3 large sprigs of basil

salt and freshly ground black pepper

175 g/6 oz Parmesan cheese, grated, to garnish

For the pasta:
1 tablespoon olive oil

375 g/12 oz fresh tagliarini

50 g/2 oz butter

salt

Fillet of Beef in Pastry with Périgourdine or Madeira Sauce

1 kg/2 lb middle-cut
fillet of beef, well trimmed

2 cloves garlic, cut into slivers

25 g/1 oz butter

1 tablespoon brandy

250 g/8 oz mushrooms, sliced

50 ml/2 fl oz port

250 g/8 oz flaky pastry

salt and freshly
ground black pepper

egg wash

For the Madeira sauce:
150 ml/¼ pint Madeira
medium or dry)

50 ml/2 fl oz brandy

25 g/1 oz butter

or 75 g/3 oz butter

300 ml/½ pint
Brown Sauce Base

beef stock (optional)

salt and freshly
ground black pepper

For the Périgourdine sauce:
1 tiny tin of truffles or
1 fresh truffle, grated

This is commonly called Beef Wellington – a very uninspiring name, reminiscent of old boots. But it is a gorgeous way to cook beef fillet, being much the juiciest. It is also the most economical – the meat is wrapped up, so there is very little evaporation and little shrinkage – you need allow only 125 g (4 oz) per person.

Make small incisions in the meat with a sharp knife, and insert the slivers of garlic. Heat the butter in a large pan until the froth begins to subside. Fry the meat, turning it to colour and flavour the outside.

Pour over the brandy, ignite and shake the pan to spread the flames. Season, then remove the meat and set aside to cool. Add the sliced mushrooms to the pan juices and gently cook through. Add the port, bring to the boil and reduce until syrupy. Season and chill.

Roll out the pastry to 3 times the width of the meat and a little longer. Place the meat at one short edge (so it will sit on the pastry join) and pile the mushrooms and buttery juices over it. Flip over the pastry and seal well all round. Brush with egg wash and keep cool until you are ready to cook it – but no longer than 4 hours.

Cook in a preheated oven at 230°C (450°F) Gas Mark 8, for about 25 minutes for pink meat or 35 minutes for well done. Serve with either a Périgourdine (truffle) or Madeira Sauce in a sauceboat.

To make the Madeira Sauce, place two-thirds of the butter in a small pan and cook over a gentle heat until it turns 'noisette' or nut-brown (about 20 minutes). Set aside. Melt the remaining butter in a pan, add the Madeira and brandy, bring to the boil and reduce by half, taking care not to let it burst into flames. Add the Brown Sauce Base, taste and adjust the seasoning and add a little beef stock if necessary to deepen the flavour. Finally beat in the browned butter.

To make the Périgourdine Sauce, chop the tinned truffles and add, with their juices, to the Madeira Sauce mixture at the same time as the Brown Sauce Base. If using a fresh truffle, add shavings of this instead.

To serve, place 2 slices of beef and pastry on each plate and serve the sauce separately.

Serves 6

Pot-roast Veal with a Rosemary-scented Sauce

A slightly sticky gravy – and easy to keep warm. Ask the butcher to cut the piece of veal from the narrow end of the cushion.

Heat the oil and butter in a non-stick casserole and brown all the vegetables. Add the veal and lightly brown on all sides, taking care not to burn the vegetables. Add the wine, bring to the boil and reduce until syrupy. Add the Brown Sauce Base, rosemary, salt and pepper, bring to the boil, cover and simmer in a preheated oven at 150°C (300°F) Gas Mark 2 for 1½ hours. Remove the lid after 1 hour.

Place the meat on a serving dish. Pour the liquid into a clean pan, remove the rosemary, bring to the boil, reduce to the thickness you prefer, and serve in a heated sauceboat. Carve the meat at the table.

Serves 6

25 ml/1 fl oz groundnut oil

25 g/1 oz butter

1 carrot, diced

10 whole baby onions

1.5 kg/3 lb veal cushion

150 ml/¼ pint dry white wine

300 ml/½ pint Brown Sauce Base

3 sprigs of rosemary

salt and freshly
ground black pepper

Braised Shin of Veal

Saffron risotto goes wonderfully well with this dish, and should be quite sticky with very little sauce. Shin of veal is the cut of meat commonly used for 'Osso Bucco', and you may see it labelled as such in butchers' shops.

Using scissors, snip the skin around the meat in several places so it stays flat as it cooks. Heat the oil in a large pan, dust the meat with the flour and fry each one until browned. Remove and keep warm.

Pour the wine into the pan, add the garlic and herbs, bring to the boil and reduce to a syrup.

Add the Brown Sauce Base, tomatoes and orange zest and bring to the boil again. Replace the meat and simmer gently for 1½ hours, or until cooked. Turn the meat occasionally to prevent it sticking, but make sure it stays on the bone. Reduce the stock if necessary.

Taste and adjust the seasoning, and serve with a saffron rice – and a spoon to extract the marrow.

Serves 6

1 tablespoon olive oil

6 slices shin of veal, about
3.5 cm/1½ inches thick

2 tablespoons plain flour

300 ml/½ pint white wine

3 garlic cloves, crushed

1 sprig of rosemary, 1 sprig of
thyme and 1 bay leaf

300 ml/½ pint Brown Sauce Base

3 tomatoes, skinned and deseeded

zest of 1 orange

salt and freshly
ground black pepper

Lamb with Pickled Peppers

Make the pepper base separately, preferably a couple of days in advance, to allow it to mature – the taste is richer after 2–3 days, but it can be used immediately. Because it's so delicious you'll have to stop marauding husbands thoughtlessly eating it all before you need it for this dish!

Two best end loins or char-grilled lamb cutlets – 2–3 per person, depending on appetite – can be substituted for the saddle. Fry them quickly in a barred griddle pan until nicely marked but still pink in the middle.

To make the Pickled Peppers, first pour all the marinade ingredients into a small pan, mix and heat through.

Halve and deseed each pepper, then cut each half into 3 pieces. Place them in a hot griddle pan until marked and browned. Cook until slightly blackened and set aside. Add the courgettes and aubergines, cook until marked and browned, and set aside.

Heat the oil in a large pan, add the celeriac and mushrooms and cook until the mushrooms are tender. Pour off the excess oil, add the peppers, courgettes and aubergines, and cook briefly to soften them a little. Add the marinade mixture and salt and pepper to taste.

Spoon into a bowl and add the balsamic vinegar. Leave the sprigs of rosemary and thyme for as long as possible, then remove the herbs and drain before serving.

To prepare the lamb, trim away any excess fat, rub the saddle with oil and season with plenty of salt and freshly ground black pepper. Roast in a preheated oven at 230°C (450°F) Gas Mark 8, for about 20 minutes. Take it out and rest in a warm place for 10 minutes.

Pour some of the fat from the lamb into a separate pan, add the vinegar and vermouth, bring to the boil and reduce until syrupy.

Add the Brown Sauce Base and stock, bring to the boil and reduce to a coating consistency. Stir in the butter and melt it into the sauce.

Reheat the pepper mixture and spoon it on to heated dinner plates. Slice the saddle of lamb parallel to the backbone in long slices. Arrange them over the peppers and pour the sauce around the meat. Garnish with the sprigs of herbs and serve.

Serves 6

1 saddle of lamb

2 tablespoons groundnut oil

75 ml/3 fl oz wine vinegar

75 ml/3 fl oz white vermouth

250 ml/8 fl oz Brown Sauce Base

150 ml/¼ pint light stock

50 g/2 oz butter

salt and pepper

sprigs of herbs, to garnish

For the pickled peppers:
3 peppers, red, yellow and green

3 courgettes, thickly sliced

2 aubergines, thickly sliced

3 tablespoons olive oil

1 celeriac, cut into batons

30 button mushrooms, quartered

50 ml/2 fl oz balsamic vinegar

salt and pepper

For the marinade:
300 ml/½ pint olive oil

1 sprig of rosemary

1 sprig of thyme

3 cloves of garlic, sliced

2 shallots, chopped

50 ml/2 fl oz sherry vinegar

Casserole of Lamb with Coriander and Ginger

1 tablespoon olive oil

1 medium onion, chopped,

2 cloves garlic, crushed

50 ml/2 fl oz white wine vinegar

500 g/1 lb tomatoes, skinned, deseeded and chopped

2 teaspoons chopped fresh ginger

1½ tablespoons chopped fresh coriander

3 lb/1.5 kg lamb, cut across the lower leg in rounds, with bone

300 ml/½ pint Brown Sauce Base

150 ml/¼ pint water

4 tablespoons crème fraîche

2 teaspoons Dijon mustard

salt and freshly ground black pepper

Accompaniment:

YOGURT SAUCE
Chop a large bunch of fresh coriander and add 1 tablespoon to 1 tub of Greek or live yogurt. Garnish with cracked black pepper and sprigs of mint.

Just as the British enjoy lamb with mint, and the French cook it with rosemary, many other countries, especially Eastern ones, prefer it with coriander. The lamb should be simmered slowly until it almost falls off the bone – a rather Moroccan flavour in fact.

I prefer the rich Greek yogurt for making the accompaniment mentioned below left, but in India and Nepal you sometimes find a delicious lemony kind called 'curd' which sets a little like junket (which Miss Muffet used to call 'curds and whey', if you remember). You can sometimes find an approximation of this lemony curd in supermarkets labelled as live set yogurt.

Heat the oil in a large pan and gently fry the onion and garlic until softened but not coloured. Add the vinegar and boil down until most of the acidity has disappeared and very little liquid remains. Add the tomatoes, ginger and coriander. Cook, stirring, until the tomato is reduced to pulp and a paste has formed.

One at a time, cook the rounds of lamb briefly in this mixture until lightly coloured, then place them in an ovenproof casserole.

Add the Brown Sauce Base to the pan and bring to the boil. Stir in all the contents of the pan, including the savoury debris. Add the water, season with salt and freshly ground black pepper and mix it all in with the lamb in the casserole. Cover and place in a preheated oven at 150°C (300°F) Gas Mark 2 for 1½ hours.

There should be about 350–450 ml/12–15 fl oz liquid remaining. If there is too much, pour it into a separate pan, bring to the boil and reduce to the required amount. Stir in the crème fraîche and mustard, then return the liquid to the casserole. Taste and adjust the seasoning and serve with boiled rice and yogurt sauce with coriander (see left).
Serves 6

Lamb with Fennel, Lemon and Anchovy Sauce

Anchovy Sauce – an Italian idea – makes a pungent change from the usual gravy, but it is unexpectedly delicious.

Fennel, with its fresh, slightly aniseed taste, has a special affinity with lamb. It is an optional accompaniment to this dish, and is also wonderful by itself as a light starter or for lunch, accompanied by good country bread and a crisp salad. If I were serving it as a solo luncheon dish, I would sprinkle it with a good layer of Parmesan cheese for the last 5 minutes of cooking time.

Rub the leg of lamb with salt, pierce it all over with a small sharp knife, and tuck pieces of garlic and rosemary into the slits. Place the leg on a rack in a roasting tin, pour in the wine and 300 ml/½ pint of the water. Place in a preheated oven at 230°C (450°F) Gas Mark 8 for 10 minutes, then reduce the heat to 150°C (300°F) Gas Mark 2 and cook for 1½ hours. Baste the joint frequently with the liquid, topping up with water as it begins to dry out and brown. (The liquid should concentrate and then be re-moistened.)

When cooked, remove the lamb to a serving dish and keep hot.

To make the baked fennel, place the fennel quarters in a single layer in a large, non-stick pan with the butter, water and a little salt. Cover and simmer until tender (approximately 15 minutes). Remove the lid, boil off the water and allow to brown a little. Place in the oven with the lamb for the last 15–20 minutes of cooking, then remove and keep warm while you prepare the anchovy sauce.

Add 150 ml/¼ pint of water to the roasting tin and scrape up all the caramelized juices sticking to the bottom. Skim off as much of the fat as possible, or pour all the liquid into a tall jug, allow the fat to float, pour it off from the top, then return the juices to the tin.

Stir in the chopped anchovies and anchovy essence, the lemon zest, parsley and Brown Sauce Base. Simmer together for a few minutes, then pour into a sauceboat and serve with the lamb. Serve with the baked fennel, if you like, or with other vegetable dishes such as Potatoes Dauphinois and a steamed green vegetable.

Serves 6

1 leg of lamb

3 garlic cloves, slivered

small sprigs of rosemary

300 ml/½ pint white wine

750 ml/1¼ pints water

salt and freshly ground black pepper

For the anchovy sauce:
½ small tin anchovies, chopped (about 6)

2 teaspoons anchovy essence

grated zest of 1 lemon

1 tablespoon chopped, fresh, flat leaf parsley

150 ml/¼ pint Brown Sauce Base

For the baked fennel (optional):
3 heads of fennel, quartered

50 g/2 oz butter

300 ml/½ pint water

salt

Breaded Lamb Cutlets with a Vermouth Sauce

175 g/6 oz butter

1 medium onion, chopped

50 g/2 oz mushrooms, chopped

1 tablespoon each of chopped fresh parsley, chervil and tarragon

150 ml/¼ pint white vermouth

300 ml/½ pint Brown Sauce Base

12 lamb cutlets

1 egg, beaten

25 g/1 oz breadcrumbs

50 g/2 oz butter, preferably clarified (see page 15)

salt and pepper

A delicious sauce for lamb – with a wonderful, very subtle suggestion of sweetness – though, strangely, it doesn't suit beef.

Heat 125 g/4 oz of the butter in a pan, add 150 ml/¼ pint water and the onion, and cook gently until the water evaporates and the onion begins to fry. Add the mushrooms, herbs and vermouth, bring to the boil and simmer until reduced and the pan is almost dry. (Do not allow to burn!) Add the Brown Sauce Base and simmer for 10 minutes.

Taste, adjust the seasoning, strain, reduce to a coating consistency and then add the remaining butter to finish, swirling it around until it melts. There should be about 375 ml/13 fl oz of sauce (add water if there isn't enough). Set aside.

Dip the cutlets first in the beaten egg, then in the breadcrumbs. Heat the butter in a separate pan and fry them on both sides. Set aside under a gentle grill, to keep warm and crisp; turn them occasionally.

To serve, spoon the sauce on to heated dinner plates and place the cutlets on top, or serve the sauce separately in a sauceboat.
Serves 6

Lamb Loin Chops with a Madeira Sauce

75 g/3 oz butter

150 ml/¼ pint Madeira

50 ml/2 fl oz brandy

12 lamb loin chops

1 tablespoon olive oil

300 ml/½ pint Brown Sauce Base

salt and freshly ground black pepper

Melt 50 g/2 oz of the butter in a large pan, remove from the heat and add the Madeira and brandy. Bring to the boil, and reduce to a syrup. Pour in the Brown Sauce Base, season with salt and lots of pepper, then beat in the rest of the butter to finish the sauce.

Meanwhile, heat the oil in a very hot pan and quickly brown the lamb chops on both sides. Remove the meat to a rack in the oven to finish cooking to your liking. Add the Madeira Sauce to the juices and simmer until it reaches a coating consistency

Place the chops or steaks on heated dinner plates, pour the sauce over, and serve with a crisp green salad.
Serves 6

Grilled Lamb Chops with a Piquant Sauce

Lamb chops are the nicest and sweetest of meats, but I think that, sometimes, a little extra zip adds to the fun. After all, variety keeps the taste buds alive and kicking.

Horseradish is very easy to grow yourself – in fact it's too easy. Unless you confine this plant in its own large pot, you will soon have a garden full to the brim with horseradish.

Place the butter, horseradish, bacon, peppercorns, chilli, nutmeg, thyme, Madeira and stock in a pan, bring to the boil and reduce to about 2 tablespoonfuls of liquid.

Add the Brown Sauce Base and the water and season with salt and freshly ground black pepper. Simmer for 30 minutes to reduce and absorb the flavours.

Cook the chops under a hot grill until browned on the outside, but still pink in the middle – or to taste.

Take the pan from under the chops, pour away the fat and stir in some of the sauce to absorb any juices. Return this mixture to the sauce in the saucepan. Bring to the boil, taste again and adjust the seasoning and, if necessary, reduce to a coating consistency.

To serve, place 3 chops on heated dinner plates, and spoon over the sauce. Suitable vegetable accompaniments would be steamed romanesco or baby patty pan squash, or tiny potatoes, boiled and then fried, and sprinkled with chopped fresh mint.

Serves 6

25 g/1 oz butter

1 tablespoon finely grated horseradish

75 g/3 oz ham or blanched bacon

12 whole black peppercorns, crushed

¼ teaspoon crushed dried chilli

¼ teaspoon grated nutmeg

1 sprig of thyme

150 ml/¼ pint Madeira

150 ml/¼ pint lamb or chicken stock

450 ml/¾ pint Brown Sauce Base

150 ml/¼ pint water

18 small lamb loin chops

salt and freshly ground black pepper

Navarin of Lamb

6 small white turnips

12 baby carrots

250 g/8 oz mangetout
or sugar snap peas

250 g/8 oz French beans

1 shoulder of lamb
or half a leg

2 tablespoon groundnut oil

1 tablespoon sugar

4 tomatoes, skinned,
deseeded and chopped

4 cloves garlic, crushed

300 ml/½ pint
Brown Sauce Base

150 ml/¼ pint water

1 sprig of thyme

1 sprig of rosemary

salt and freshly
ground black pepper

A wonderful dish – just as good for a grand dinner party as for cosy family gatherings. We used to put it in a wide-necked vacuum flask when we went to the seaside. It would finish cooking while we bathed! (On such occasions we left out the vegetables.) It takes a bit longer to cook that way and must be boiling when you put into the flask – but it is very good with just a crusty bread and a light red wine to hold up against the sparkling blue of the sea.

Although everyone thinks of Navarin as a springtime dish – and so it is in parts of France – in Britain, it is really a dish of early to midsummer, when the vegetables are tiny and sweet, but not yet bursting into full maturity. However, these days, when we import fruits and vegetables from all over the world, we have small, sweet vegetables at any time of year.

Little onions and baby potatoes are sometimes added too, and steamed radishes are pretty. It is possible that the name 'navarin' comes from the French word for turnip, 'navet', so on no account leave them out.

Lightly steam or boil the vegetables, refresh and set aside.

Cut the lamb into 2.5 cm/1 inch cubes and discard the fat and bone. Heat the oil in a non-stick pan and brown the meat on all sides. Sprinkle it with the sugar, heating and stirring it until the sugar caramelizes. Add the tomatoes and garlic and simmer for 5 minutes. Add the Brown Sauce Base and water, herbs and seasoning.

Pour into a large ovenproof casserole, bring to the boil, cover and simmer gently in a preheated oven at 150°C (300°F) Gas Mark 2 for about 40 minutes or until the meat is tender.

Pour off the juices into a clean pan, bring to the boil and reduce them if they have become too liquid.

Add the cooked turnips, carrots, peas and beans to the casserole, and reheat gently in the oven for 10 minutes. Mix gently, taste and adjust the seasoning, and serve.

Serves 6

Veal Escalopes with Creamy Mushrooms

500 g/1 lb closed button mushrooms

300 ml/½ pint duck stock (defatted), or other good, homemade stock

1 tablespoon lemon juice

150 ml/¼ pint whipping cream

1 egg yolk

75 g/3 oz butter

6 veal escalopes, lightly seasoned

150 ml/¼ pint white wine

450 ml/¾ pint Brown Sauce Base

150 ml/¼ pint duck or chicken stock

6 small slices of ham, sliced from the bone

salt and freshly ground black pepper

If you have any duck stock made from a roast carcass, keep it for this dish. It gives the Brown Sauce an extra depth – and indeed any homemade stock will always enrich the Brown Sauce Base. Serve this dish with a bright green vegetable, such as broccoli or green beans.

Place the mushrooms in a pan with the duck stock, lemon juice and a little salt. Cover and simmer for about 5 minutes, until heated through. Strain, put the mushrooms aside, and reserve the stock.

Bring the stock to the boil and reduce to about 150 ml/¼ pint of concentrated liquid, then stir in the cream and reduce to a coating consistency. Return the mushrooms to the pan, add the egg yolk and set aside to keep warm.

Melt the butter in a large frying pan, and cook the veal escalopes very gently – really little more than just heating them through. Remove the veal to a flameproof dish, add the ham slices, season with salt and freshly ground black pepper, and set aside to keep warm.

Bring the juices to the boil and allow them to darken and caramelize. Add the wine and reduce to 2 teaspoons (until you can see the oily butter again). Add the Brown Sauce Base and the stock, bring to the boil and reduce to 450 ml/¾ pint.

Bring the cream sauce back to the boil, add the mushrooms, their juices and the egg yolk. Stir well and keep warm.

Place the veal under the grill to heat, or in a preheated oven at 240°C (475°F) Gas Mark 9.

Arrange the veal and ham on a large serving platter. Spoon the mushrooms in their creamy sauce into the middle, add any juices to the brown sauce mixture, taste and adjust the seasoning, then pour over the meat.

Alternatively, divide both the meats between heated dinner plates, spoon the creamy mushrooms beside and then drizzle the brown sauce over and beside.

Serves 6

Pork or Veal Cutlets in Sage and Garlic Sauce with Cèpes

Dried cèpes or porcini are now widely available if you can't obtain fresh wild mushrooms; they will give a very strong, characteristic flavour to this dish.

This can be quite expensive when made with veal, but is equally good with pork. Use neck end pork cutlets which can be simmered until tender without drying out.

Pour 1 cup of boiling water over the dried cèpes and leave to soak for 20 minutes. Strain and reserve the liquid, and treat the cèpes as fresh.

Heat the butter and oil in a large frying pan, and add the garlic. Dry the cèpes (or wipe them if fresh), slice them and fry them gently in the pan. Season, remove with a slotted spoon and keep warm.

In the same oil, brown the cutlets on both sides and place them in a large casserole. Pour off excess fat from the pan, then add the sage or rosemary, the thyme and shallots. Pour in the wine, bring to the boil and reduce until syrupy. Add the Brown Sauce Base, the chicken or veal stock and the cèpe liquid, if using dried cèpes. Stir well, season to taste, and pour over the cutlets.

Cover the casserole, bring to the boil and simmer gently for about 1½ hours until the pork is tender – or a bit less if you are using veal.

Remove the cutlets on to a serving plate and keep warm. Check the liquid content of the dish, which should have increased considerably. If there is a lot of fat on the top, spoon off as much as you can, using kitchen paper, if necessary, to absorb it. Bring the liquid to the boil and reduce to a coating consistency.

Pour the sauce over the cutlets, sprinkle with the cocktail gherkins or cornichons, if using, and serve.

Serves 6

1 tablespoon dried cèpes, or porcini, or 2–3 fresh ones, sliced

50 g/2 oz butter

50 ml/2 fl oz groundnut oil

3 cloves of garlic, crushed

6 neck end pork cutlets, or veal cutlets

3–4 sage leaves, chopped or 1 tablespoon chopped fresh rosemary leaves

½ tablespoon chopped fresh thyme leaves

3 shallots, chopped

300 ml/½ pint white wine

350 ml/12 fl oz Brown Sauce Base

350 ml/12 fl oz chicken or veal stock, or water

salt and freshly ground black pepper

3 cocktail gherkins or 10 small French cornichons, chopped, to garnish (optional)

Pork Chops in Brown Vermouth Sauce

50 ml/2 fl oz groundnut oil

6 pork chops, with excess fat removed

2 cloves of garlic, sliced

3 sprigs of sage or rosemary

1 bay leaf

175 g/6 fl oz white vermouth

500 g/1 lb tomatoes, deseeded

1 tablespoon white wine vinegar

1 teaspoon sugar

300 ml/½ pint Brown Sauce Base

1 tablespoon finely chopped gherkins

1 tablespoon capers

salt and freshly ground black pepper

Pork always has an unfortunate tendency to dry out during cooking, especially if the oven temperature is too high. Ideally the meat should never reach boiling point, as protein cooks well below 100°C but above about 70°C, allowing about 30°C leeway. The solution is just to braise it very slowly for a long time.

Vermouth is a useful ingredient in cooking. It provides all the advantages of white wine, but it also already contains the essences of thirty-six herbs, so much of the flavour-adding work has already been done for you. I always use the French Noilly Prat, because I find that the Italian brands are sharper and more astringent. You may like to try this yourself – reduce separate pans of each and do the taste test to see which one you prefer.

Heat the oil in a large pan and brown the chops on both sides, then transfer them to an ovenproof casserole. Pour off the fat from the pan, add the garlic, herbs and white vermouth, bring to the boil and reduce until syrupy.

Place the tomatoes, vinegar and sugar into a liquidizer or food processor and purée until smooth. Pour the mixture into the pan, bring to the boil and reduce until the tomatoes begin to fry.

Add the Brown Sauce Base, bring to the boil, season and pour over the chops. Cover and cook in a preheated oven at 140°C (275°F) Gas Mark 1 for about 40–45 minutes.

Place the chops on heated dinner plates and keep warm. Remove any fat from the sauce with a spoon and kitchen paper. Bring the sauce to the boil and reduce if necessary. Taste and adjust the seasoning. Pour over the chops, then sprinkle over the chopped gherkins and capers.

Serves 6

Pork Chops in Red Wine and Marsala Sauce

Pork is one of those meats traditionally paired with sweet sauces or other ingredients. Sweetness, in the form of fruit, honey or sweet wines like Marsala, was added to dishes with fatty meats like pork, goose or duck. Modern pork is, of course, nowhere near as fatty as it once was, but the tradition lives on.

For some reason, pork chops can sometimes be impossibly tough. Test the meat after 20 minutes, and if you find it is a little chewy, you can solve the problem by returning them to the pan with the Brown Sauce Base for another 40 minutes.

This will change the dish into a type of casserole and there would therefore be no need to strain out the garlic and fennel seeds.

This sauce is also delicious with other meats, such as chicken thighs (the joint with the best flavour), veal cutlets or lamb butterfly chops.

Cut away the rind and excess fat from the chops. Mix the garlic with the salt and the olive oil and smear liberally over the meat. Place in the refrigerator for about 2 hours to absorb the flavours.

Heat a non-stick pan until hot, and brown the chops on both sides. Pour off the excess fat and lower the heat. Continue to cook the chops for a further 20 minutes, turning them over half way. Remove them to a dish with their juices and keep warm.

Pour the Marsala and wine into the hot pan, sprinkle in the fennel seeds, bring to the boil and reduce until syrupy. Mix in the tomato purée and Brown Sauce Base and return the meat juices to the pan.

Simmer until well mixed, then taste and adjust the seasoning, and reduce to a coating consistency.

To serve, place the pork chops on heated dinner plates, and pour over the sauce. The delicious vegetable dish, right, of spinach, water chestnuts and nutmeg, is a suitable accompaniment.

Serves 6

6 pork chops,

3 cloves of garlic, crushed

½ teaspoon salt

50 ml/2 fl oz olive oil

50 ml/2 fl oz Marsala

175 ml/6 fl oz light red wine

½ teaspoon fennel seeds

2 teaspoons tomato purée

300 ml/½ pint Brown Sauce Base

salt and freshly ground black pepper

Accompaniment:

SPINACH WITH NUTMEG AND WATER CHESTNUTS

Wash the spinach, tear it into pieces and place in a large covered pan with a little butter. While the spinach is sweating, chop 6 water chestnuts and add to the pan with about ¼ teaspoon of grated nutmeg. Stir and serve.

Oxtail in Burgundy Sauce

Slow cooking is essential for this dish to taste really good. It takes two to three hours to achieve a good oxtail Burgundy base and the dish then needs up to eight hours, or overnight in a slow cooker after that, or about four hours gently simmering in an ordinary oven.

Choose a large tail and use the biggest pieces. Ask your butcher to cut carefully between the segments, or do it yourself with a small, sharp knife – don't allow him to chop with a cleaver.

To make the sauce, heat half the oil in a large pan add the shallots and cook until lightly browned. Add the smaller pieces of oxtail and cook until lightly browned on all sides. Add the wine and half the brandy, bring to the boil and reduce until syrupy. Pour in the Brown Sauce Base and simmer for 2–3 hours.

To cook the larger pieces of oxtail, heat the remaining oil in a non-stick pan, and brown the pieces, 3 at a time. Pour away any fat. Return the meat to the pan and sprinkle with thyme and garlic. Pour the remaining brandy over the meat and ignite, shaking the pan until the flames die down. Transfer the meat to a slow cooker or ovenproof casserole dish. Deglaze with 1 cup of water and add to the casserole.

Bring the Burgundy Sauce to the boil and strain it into the slow cooker or casserole.

Cover the slow cooker and keep the temperature between 80–90°C for up to 6 hours or overnight. Blot the surface with kitchen paper if there is any fat floating on the top when you remove the lid.

If using a casserole, bring to the boil on top of the stove, then cover and place in a very low oven, preheated to 150°C (300°F) Gas Mark 2 and cook for 4–6 hours. The liquid should not boil, just barely shiver.

Place the oxtail pieces on heated plates. Correct the consistency of the sauce by either boiling and reducing, or by adding more liquid. Pour over the oxtail and serve with creamy mashed potatoes mixed with chopped fresh flat-leaf parsley and a green vegetable in season, such as steamed baby fennel.

Serves 6

2 tablespoons groundnut oil

6 shallots, chopped

2 large oxtails, trimmed of fat

1 bottle red Burgundy

125 ml/4 fl oz brandy

**900 ml/1½ pints
Brown Sauce Base**

**1 tablespoon chopped
fresh thyme leaves**

1 clove of garlic, crushed

**salt and freshly
ground black pepper**

Note:
SLOW COOKERS
These were fashionable some years ago, but can sometimes be difficult to find now. They are invaluable for making stocks, the Brown Sauce Base or any other long, slow-cooked dishes.

Lambs' Tongues in Madeira Sauce

24 pickled lambs' tongues

1 celery stick, finely sliced

1 small leek, finely sliced

¼ small fennel bulb, sliced (optional)

125 g/4 oz butter

25 ml/1 fl oz brandy

25 ml/1 fl oz Madeira

275 ml/9 fl oz
Brown Sauce Base

150 ml/¼ pint light stock

12 small vol-au-vent cases

salt and freshly
ground black pepper

mixed green salad leaves
with vinaigrette, to garnish

If the lambs' tongues are pickled by the butcher for three days before cooking, they have an appetizing colour and a delicious, delicate flavour. You must order them in advance, however, since they are only pickled to order. Serve them as a starter garnished with chervil.

A delicious alternative – suitable for serving as a main course – is to prepare the broad beans as in the recipe for Pickled Pork on page 88, or the Olive Mash of potatoes and celeriac on page 116, and pile in the centre of heated dinner plates. Slice the cooked lambs' tongues lengthways and arrange on top of the broad beans or mash. Pour the sauce over and around, and garnish with sprigs of chervil or flat leaf parsley, or a few whole broad beans, popped out of their grey coats, and scattered over the plate.

Rinse the tongues and tidy them up a bit with a pair of scissors. Place in a pan with the vegetables and cold water to cover, bring to the boil and simmer slowly for about 2 hours. Lift out the tongues and, when they are cool enough to handle, remove any gristle and bony bits, and very carefully peel off the skins. Strain and reserve the cooking liquid.

Meanwhile, place half the butter in a pan and heat very slowly until it browns. Set aside.

Pour the brandy and Madeira into another pan with the remaining butter, bring to the boil and reduce by half. Pour in the Brown Sauce Base and the stock, bring to the boil again and simmer gently until reduced by half.

Add the reserved cooking liquid to the sauce to help season and flavour it. Bring to the boil again, reduce to a coating consistency then beat in the browned butter.

To serve, heat the vol-au-vent cases and place on heated starter plates, slice the tongues into 1 cm/½ inch cubes, heat them in the sauce and spoon into the cases. Serve, garnished with a little salad of mixed green salad leaves, dressed with vinaigrette.

Serves 6

Lambs' Kidneys in Mustard Sauce

One of the great British breakfast dishes   traditionally served with toast. Serve it with mashed potatoes for a more substantial meal.

Heat the butter in a heavy-based pan and fry the bacon gently until browned. Remove and drain on kitchen paper.

Fry the kidneys, round-side down, and gently simmer until three-quarters cooked. Turn over and finish cooking so no blood shows. Do not overcook.

Remove from the pan and set aside, with the bacon, in a warm place.

Add the mustard to the pan and scrape up any brown bits. Add the Brown Sauce Base and freshly ground black pepper, and simmer for a few minutes to blend the flavours. Serve with toast or olive-mashed potatoes (see page 116).

Serves 6

75 g/3 oz butter

2 rashers thick-cut,
sweet-cure bacon, cut
into 5 mm/¼ inch strips

9 lambs' kidneys,
halved and cored

1 tablespoon German mustard

275 ml/9 fl oz Brown Sauce Base

freshly ground black pepper

Pig's Liver in Sage Sauce

A recipe with rather a lot of delicious port and brandy, so be careful when you reduce the alcohol. Turn off any naked flame (including the gas) as you pour it into the pan, since you don't want to flambé this lot! It really does make a difference to the depth of the flavour of the sauce although you can omit it altogether and rely on the sage and seasoning. Serve with lots of mashed potato – but not bacon.

Mix the flour with salt, pepper and the sage, and use it to dust the liver slices. Heat the oil and butter in a large pan and quickly fry the liver, then remove and keep warm.

Turn off the flame, remove the pan from the heat and carefully pour in the alcohol. Return to the beat, bring to the boil and reduce to about 2 tablespoons. Add the thyme, lots of pepper and the Brown Sauce Base, reheat to simmering, taste and adjust the seasoning.

Return the liver to the pan and gently baste with the sauce for a few minutes to reheat and coat the meat. Take care not to cook it further. Serve on heated dinner plates with creamy mashed potatoes.

Serves 6

2 tablespoons flour

1 tablespoon chopped
fresh sage leaves

750 g/1½ lb pig's liver, skinned,
trimmed of all tubes, then sliced

1 tablespoon groundnut oil

25 g/1 oz butter

75 ml/3 fl oz port

75 ml/3 fl oz brandy

1 teaspoon chopped
fresh thyme leaves

300 ml/½ pint Brown Sauce Base

salt and freshly
ground black pepper

Individual Cassoulets

500 g/1 lb smoked
gammon in a piece

2 tablespoons olive oil

125 g/4 oz fresh
breadcrumbs

6 cloves of garlic, crushed

1 tablespoon chopped
fresh flat leaf parsley

750 g/1½ lb lamb,
cut from the shoulder

750 g/1½ lb belly of pork,
without rind

4 tomatoes, skinned,
deseeded and chopped

1 teaspoon tomato purée

1 sprig of thyme

1 bay leaf

300 ml/½ pint
Brown Sauce Base

250 g/8 oz garlic sausage

375 g/12 oz dried
cannellini beans, soaked
and cooked to produce about
1.25 kg/2½ lb cooked beans

salt and freshly
ground black pepper

This is the perfect dish to eat in front of an open fire with lots of red wine on a cold winter's evening. Usually a cassoulet is made in one big pot but cooking it individually this way means that everyone gets lots of the breadcrumb crust and the beans stay juicy and moist right to the very last mouthful.

You can prepare the beans yourself by soaking them overnight, then simmering gently on top of the stove until done (the time will depend on the age of the beans). Otherwise, you can use the very good canned cannellini beans from Italy. Use more beans if you like your cassoulet very 'beany' – though I must admit I prefer mine more meaty, garlicky and crumby.

Place the gammon in a saucepan, cover with water, bring to the boil and simmer until tender (about 45 minutes).

Heat half the oil in a pan, add the breadcrumbs, 2 of the garlic cloves and the parsley. Fry gently until browned, then set aside.

Cut the lamb and belly of pork into rough cubes. Heat the remaining oil in a non-stick pan, and brown the meat on all sides. Add the remaining garlic cloves, tomatoes, tomato purée, thyme and bay leaf. Pour in the Brown Sauce Base and add some of the gammon water to cover. Bring to the boil, cover and simmer for 35 minutes.

Cut the gammon and garlic sausage into evenly-sized pieces and add to the pan. Bring to the boil again and simmer for another 15 minutes. Taste and adjust the seasoning, then strain the meat, reserving the cooking liquid.

Fill 6 individual dishes with alternate layers of beans and the meats.

Pour in the sauce liquid until the layers are almost covered. Bring any remaining sauce to the boil, reduce, and top up the dishes with it. Sprinkle over the breadcrumb mixture and place in a preheated oven at 230°C (450°F) Gas Mark 8, for 35 minutes, or until the crumbs have a rich colour and have soaked up some of the juices.

This dish needs no accompaniment other than a crisp green salad of mixed leaves with a mustardy vinaigrette – and plenty of red wine.

Serves 6

Pheasant in Red Wine

Do not overcook young pheasant as it becomes very dry. If necessary, carve off the breast as soon as it is done and continue cooking the legs a little longer.

I must say that supermarket pheasants are usually old birds, and should be cooked longer – perhaps an extra twenty-five minutes.

You can vary this dish by using white wine instead of red.

Rub the pheasants all over with half the oil and some salt. Heat the butter in a heavy-based non-stick frying pan and brown the birds on all sides, cooking for about 20 minutes.

Heat the remaining oil in a deep non-stick casserole pan and fry the bacon, onion, garlic, celery and herbs until lightly browned. Add the red wine, Madeira and brandy, bring to the boil and reduce until syrupy. Add the Brown Sauce Base. Place the birds on top of the sauce and cook in a preheated oven at 200°C (400°F) Gas Mark 6, for another 20 minutes.

Remove the pheasants and carve off the legs and breasts. Cut the legs in half and slice the breasts.

Strain the sauce through a sieve into a gravy boat.

Lay the celery, bacon and onion on a heated serving dish, place the pieces of leg and breast on top, and garnish with triangles of fried bread. Alternatively, spoon the bacon and vegetable mixture on to heated dinner plates, place the pheasant beside, garnish with the bread triangles and pour the sauce around.

Fried apple rings, as in the recipe for Barbary Duck on page 114, is also a delicious accompaniment for the pheasant.

Serves 6

2 young pheasants

2 tablespoons groundnut oil

50 g/2 oz butter

50 g/2 oz streaky bacon

1 onion, chopped

1 clove of garlic, crushed

2 celery sticks, chopped

2 tablespoons chopped, fresh, flat leaf parsley

1 tablespoon chopped fresh thyme leaves, or 1 teaspoon dried

1 bay leaf

150 ml/¼ pint red wine

50 ml/2 fl oz Madeira

50 ml/2 fl oz brandy

300 ml/½ pint Brown Sauce Base

salt and freshly ground black pepper

12 triangles of fried bread, to garnish (3 slices)

Pithivier of Pheasant

50 g/2 oz butter

1 clove of garlic, crushed

1 teaspoon chopped
fresh thyme leaves

1 onion, chopped

75 ml/3 fl oz white wine

150 ml/¼ pint port

150 ml/¼ pint stock

4 pheasant legs and
1 pheasant breast,
cut into 1 cm/½ inch dice

4 tablespoons breadcrumbs

375 g/12 oz shortcrust
pastry, rolled

6 strips smoked back bacon

egg wash, to glaze

salt and freshly
ground black pepper

For the Madeira sauce:
600 ml/1 pint chicken
or veal stock

150 ml/¼ pint port

150 ml/¼ pint Madeira

150 ml/¼ pint
Brown Sauce Base

25 g/1 oz butter, to finish

This dish and its sauce complement each other so well that it is hard to imagine one without the other. Thus it comes as a happy surprise to discover how very good the pithivier tastes when eaten later, by itself, cold. Try it on a picnic.

Use a small, deep bowl, such as a Chinese tea bowl, perhaps 5 cm/2 inches deep and 6 cm/2½ inches in diameter, as the pithivier mould (you'll only need one).

Heat the butter in a small pan. Sauté the garlic, thyme and onion until softened but not coloured. Add the wine and port, bring to the boil and reduce by half. Add stock, bring to the boil, and reduce to a glaze.

Remove the meat from the pheasant legs, trimming and discarding any sinews. Place the meat from the legs, and the reduced glaze, in a liquidizer or food processor and purée until smooth.

Turn out into a bowl, then stir in the breadcrumbs to mop up any liquid and give a sausagemeat-like consistency. Season to taste.

Roll out the pastry and cut 2 rounds per person, one to line the small Chinese tea bowl, and one to form the lid.

Line the bowl with the large round, and fill, first with an eye from the rasher of bacon, then with the pheasant mix interspersed with the diced pieces of pheasant breast. Reserve the rest of the bacon for another use.

Top the bowl with the smaller pastry round and brush over with egg wash. Turn out the pithivier, upside down on to a plate, and pinch the edges firmly together, marking them with the traditional pattern, as in the photograph, right). Brush over with the egg wash. Repeat with the remaining pastry and pheasant mixture until you have 6 pithiviers.

Make a hole in the top, and cook in a preheated oven at about 180°C (350°F) Gas Mark 4 for 25 minutes or until golden.

To make the sauce, chop up the carcass and brown in the oven. Place in a pan, add stock, boil then simmer for 40 minutes and strain.

Pour the port and Madeira into a clean saucepan, bring to the boil and reduce to a syrup. Add the pheasant stock, bring to the boil again and reduce to about 450 ml/¾ pint. Add the Brown Sauce Base and beat in the butter to finish the sauce.

Spoon the finished sauce on to heated dinner plates and place a pithivier in the centre of each.

Serves 6

Hare in Red Wine

2 tablespoons olive oil

4 hare legs, jointed

2 tablespoons brandy

350 ml/12 fl oz red wine

1 teaspoon dried thyme

300 ml/½ pint
Brown Sauce Base

250 g/8 oz thick-sliced
bacon, cubed

125 g/4 oz large
mushrooms, quartered

150 ml/¼ pint soured cream

salt and freshly
ground black pepper

For the herb dumplings:
150 ml/¼ pint water

40 g/1½ oz butter

¼ teaspoon nutmeg

zest and juice of 1 lemon

50 g/2 oz flour

1 tablespoon chopped
fresh flat leaf parsley

1 tablespoon chopped
fresh thyme leaves

2 eggs

salt

Hare legs have a remarkable amount of very good meat on them; two legs will easily feed three people. This recipe has soured cream added to finish the sauce, thus removing some of the very strong hare flavour. Use the saddles in another recipe, such as Roast Saddle of Hare in a Creamy Sauce (page 91). The Herb Dumplings are also delicious with the Pot-au-feu on page 44.

To make the Herb Dumplings, pour the water into a saucepan, add the butter, nutmeg, lemon zest and salt to taste. Bring to the boil, then stir in the flour and cook until it forms a ball.

Spoon into a liquidizer or food processor, add lemon juice, herbs and eggs and process until well mixed. Beat the mixture into the flour mixture to form choux paste. Drop teaspoons of the paste into a large pan of boiling water and poach until firm. Set aside to keep warm.

Heat half the oil in a deep, heavy-based pan and fry the hare legs for a few minutes, to stiffen them. Pour the brandy over the hare, ignite and shake the pan to spread the flames.

Remove the meat from the pan, add the wine and thyme, bring to the boil and reduce until syrupy. Add the Brown Sauce Base, bring to the boil, return the meat to the pan and allow to simmer.

Meanwhile, place the cubed bacon in a small pan, cover with plain water, and bring to the boil. Drain and rinse the bacon under running water, then add to the simmering mixture.

Heat the remaining oil in a small pan and fry the mushrooms until lightly browned. Add to the meat and continue to simmer until the hare is tender, about 45 minutes. Remove the meat, divide into bite-sized pieces and set aside to keep warm.

Pour the soured cream into the pan and mix well. Taste and adjust the seasoning, then bring to the boil, reduce to a coating consistency and return the meat to the pan to heat through.

Place the meat in a heated serving dish, pour the sauce over, and serve with the Herb Dumplings.

Serves 6

Venison Pie

Years ago this dish was given to me by a friend in Scotland and I always found that the orange zest gave a startling twist to the usual flavour of game pie. Since then, I've noticed that the French often add dried orange peel to stews. Scotland and France still have a good deal in common. Vive the 'Auld Alliance'!

Cut the bacon into bite-sized pieces. Heat the oil in a large pan, add the bacon and venison and fry until browned. Fry in small batches, or the meat will release too much liquid and boil in its own juices. The idea is to brown and caramelize those juices so they coat the outsides of the meat, adding to the taste of the finished dish. The saltpetre in the bacon turns the venison a beautiful and very appetizing red.

Lift out each batch of meat when browned and mix well in a large pie dish, 1.8 litre/3 pint capacity.

Pour the red wine into the pan, bring to the boil and reduce until syrupy. Stir in the tomato purée, orange zest, marjoram and Brown Sauce Base. Simmer for 5 minutes, taste and adjust the seasoning. Pour this sauce over the meat in the pie dish, mix well and cover with foil. Place in a preheated oven at 150°C (300°F) Gas Mark 2 for about 1½ hours, or until the meat is tender.

Remove the dish from the oven, strain the juices into a pan and return the meat to the pie dish. Bring the juices to the boil, reduce until you have a sauce-like consistency and pour it over the meat.

Roll out the shortcrust pastry to about 5 mm/¼ inch thick and big enough to fit the top of the pie dish. Brush the rim of the dish with water, and place the pastry over the top, crimping the edges with your fingers or a fork. Trim off any extra pastry, re-roll and cut out pastry leaves to decorate the top.

Brush the top of the pie with the beaten egg, arrange the pastry leaves on top and brush them with beaten egg. Cook in a preheated oven at 220°C (425°F) Gas Mark 7, for about 25 minutes or until cooked and golden brown.

Serves 6

500 g/1 lb green bacon in the piece, rind removed (must be saltpetre-cured)

2 tablespoons groundnut oil

1.25 kg/2½ lb venison from the leg, cut into bite-sized cubes

300 ml/½ pint red wine

1 tablespoon tomato purée

zest of 1 orange

1 tablespoon chopped fresh marjoram leaves

600 ml/1 pint Brown Sauce Base

375 g/12 oz shortcrust pastry for the top

1 egg, beaten, to glaze

salt and freshly ground black pepper

Venison Noisettes Grand Veneur

6 venison noisettes, about
125 g/4 oz each (with a smaller
animal buy 12–18 noisettes)

300 ml/½ pint
Brown Sauce Base

50 g/2 oz butter

50 ml/2 fl oz brandy

150 ml/¼ pint red wine

1 teaspoon
Worcestershire sauce

salt and lots of freshly
ground black pepper

For the marinade:
50 ml/¼ pint red wine

1 teaspoon dried thyme

1 small onion, chopped

1 tablespoon groundnut oil

For the chestnut purée:
500 g/1 lb fresh chestnuts

milk and water, to cover

450 ml/¾ pint whipping cream

salt and pepper

To serve:
6 round slices of white
bread slightly larger than the
noisettes, fried in butter

50 g/2 oz pine nuts, fried
in butter until golden brown

sprigs of thyme (optional)

Quite possibly the most delicious way of serving any kind of venison. The marinade not only tenderizes the meat and enhances its flavour; it is also the most important ingredient of the gorgeous Grand Veneur Sauce, the richness of which is perfectly counterbalanced by the plain sweetness of the chestnut purée – itself an indispensable ingredient (and delicious with many other dishes in this book, such as the Roast Saddle of Hare in a Creamy Sauce, on page 91.

Pour all the marinade ingredients into a pan, boil until syrupy, then add 150 ml/¼ pint water. Add the meat, cover and leave overnight.

Next day, remove and dry the meat. Pour the marinade into a pan, bring to the boil and reduce by half. Add the Brown Sauce Base, bring to the boil, simmer for 15 minutes and strain.

Heat the butter in a large pan and sauté the marinated noisettes until browned on both sides. Remove the pan from the heat, pour the brandy over the meat, ignite and shake the pan to spread the flames. Remove the meat and keep warm.

Pour the red wine into the pan, bring to the boil, reduce until syrupy, then add the Brown Sauce Base mixture. Add lots of freshly ground black pepper and the Worcestershire sauce. Taste and adjust the seasoning, bring to the boil and reduce until thick and sticky.

To prepare the chestnuts, drop them in boiling water until the shells soften. Cut in half and take the flesh out of the shells, removing as much fibre as possible. Return to the rinsed saucepan and cover with half-and-half milk and water. Simmer for about 30 minutes. Place the chestnuts and milk mixture in a liquidizer or food processor and purée until smooth. Season with salt and pepper, then stir in the cream.

Place the fried croûtes on heated dinner plates, top with the warmed chestnut purée and the venison. Pour the sauce around, sprinkle the toasted pine kernels and thyme sprigs (if using) over the top and serve.
Serves 6

sugar
SAUCE BASE

A SIMPLE MIXTURE of sugar and water, this Sugar Sauce Base is, like the others, very easy to make – just sugar and water, boiled until clear.

It is made in a minute, and is much more versatile that one might expect. You would of course expect to find Sugar Syrup in recipes for sorbets, ices and puddings of all kinds, but you can also use it in recipes for starters, meats and traditional accompaniments such as Glazed Onions and Onion Confit on page 164.

Make it in quantity and keep it in a loose-topped jar in the fridge – it will keep for at least a month – and you'll find that, since you have it on hand, you'll use it much more often.

You can also cook the syrup on to form a caramel, or even further until it becomes even darker. Pour the dark mixture on to a sheet of foil, then cool and crack or crumble it, and use it as a crunchy topping for recipes such as the Ginger Crème Brûlée on page 92.

1 Pour the water into a saucepan, then add the sugar. Bring to the boil over a gentle heat.

This is, without doubt, the simplest of all the sauce bases – just sugar and water boiled together until the sugar dissolves completely. The syrup is enormously versatile, and can be used in many different ways – and not just in puddings and desserts, where you would most expect to find it.

TO MAKE 600 ML/1 PINT

300 ml/½ pint water
425 g/14 oz sugar

1 Pour the water into a saucepan, then add the sugar, and bring to the boil

2 Stir the sugar and water together until the sugar has dissolved.

3 Bring to the boil and boil gently until clear.

The Sugar Syrup can then be stored in an airtight container in the refrigerator and used as required.

2 Stir the sugar and water together until the sugar has dissolved.

TO MAKE A THICKER SYRUP

Boil a little longer. A possible problem is that the sugar may crystallize when bits stick to the side of the pan and dry out. Just add water and start again.

THE SOFT BALL STAGE

Let a few drops of syrup fall into a bowl of cold water, where it will go into a chewy lump.

TO MAKE CARAMEL

Simmer the syrup gently until it turns the required colour. Dip the base of the pan into cold water for a moment to halt the browning of the sugar.

THE CRACK STAGE

Boil the syrup longer until strings pull from it and solidify into stiff threads.

3 Bring to the boil and boil gently until clear. When ready, the Sugar Syrup can be stored in an airtight container in the refrigerator.

Icy Tomato Soup

175 g/6 fl oz sherry vinegar

125 ml/4 fl oz olive oil

2 shallots, chopped

125 ml/4 fl oz
Sugar Syrup Sauce Base

1 kg/2 lb tomatoes, skinned
and deseeded with skin
and seeds retained

2 sprigs of basil

salt and freshly
ground black pepper

6 small sprigs of basil,
to garnish

Alternatively:

TOMATO ICE-CREAM
Skin, chop and cook 1 kg/2 lb
tomatoes in 300 ml/½ pint
Sugar Syrup Sauce Base.
Liquidize, then pass through a
sieve. Return to the liquidizer
and blend in 250 g/8 oz
mascarpone. Freeze as in the
sorbet recipes on pages 171–3.
If you would like a stronger
tomato flavour, mix in
1 teaspoon tomato purée
before freezing.

A delicious and unusual soup – a cross between a sorbet and a soup – wonderful and cooling for a hot summer's day.

The texture is interesting – quite thick, like a Cream of Tomato Soup, and a rather creamy colour, too. It should be ice-cold – but without any ice-crystals, and certainly not solidifying. You can make it the day before and freeze it, but make sure it is thoroughly thawed, but still ice-cold, before serving.

A Tomato Granita is an alternative use for this recipe. Make it as in the main recipe, add 2 egg whites, churn in a sorbetière or follow the freezing instructions on pages 171 or 173 for the Melon or Nectarine Sorbets. Serve it between courses as a palate-cleanser, or as a first course, garnished with sprigs of basil or mint.

Pour the vinegar and half the oil into a non-metal or stainless steel pan, add the shallots, bring to the boil and reduce until the vinegar has been absorbed into the shallots. Add the Sugar Syrup Sauce Base and the skins, pips and juices from the tomatoes. Simmer for 5 minutes, strain and add to the tomato flesh, then add the basil and remaining oil. Pour into a liquidizer or food processor and purée until smooth. Taste and adjust the seasoning. Chill the soup until icy cold but not solidifying, then serve in chilled soup bowls, garnished with small sprigs of basil.

If made in advance and frozen solid, take out of the freezer and allow 2 hours in the refrigerator for the ice to melt.

Serves 6

Orange Vinaigrette with Pears and Cheese

150 ml/¼ pint Sugar Syrup Sauce Base

150 ml/¼ pint white wine vinegar

150 ml/¼ pint water

grated zest of 1 orange

1 teaspoon Dijon mustard

150 ml/¼ pint groundnut oil

3 large, ripe dessert pears

250 g/8 oz full-cream cheese

½ teaspoon paprika

mixed green salad leaves, to garnish

This is an American recipe with an orange difference – a cool and delicious starter for lunch or dinner, which could also be made with a low-fat cheese if you prefer.

An interesting alternative is to drizzle 1 whole head of garlic per person with good olive oil and bake until soft and nutty. Serve with 2 slices of young chèvre, lambs' lettuce and rocket, and spoon over the vinaigrette. Sprinkle with flakes of sea salt and cracked black pepper.

Pour the Sugar Syrup Sauce Base into a heavy-based pan and boil down until golden and caramelized. Add the vinegar, and boil down to 150 ml/¼ pint. Add the water and orange zest, reduce to 150 ml/¼ pint, then mix in 1 teaspoon Dijon mustard. Do not stir the mixture but let it dissolve on its own by fast boiling. Pour into a wide-necked jar, add the oil, screw on the lid and shake hard to emulsify. Chill.

Peel the pears, cut in half lengthways and cut a sliver off the back of each half to make a flat base. Scoop out the cores and fill the cavities with the cream cheese. Place the pears on starter plates, surrounded with green salad leaves. Sprinkle with paprika and pour over the orange vinaigrette just before serving.

Serves 6

Raspberry Vinaigrette

250 g/8 oz raspberries, fresh or frozen

150 ml/¼ pint Sugar Syrup Sauce Base

25 ml/1 fl oz white wine vinegar

150 ml/¼ pint groundnut oil

freshly ground black pepper

The colour of this delicious sauce is electrifying! Use it with avocado and prawns or with smoked salmon mousse, where the tartness cuts the oiliness of the salmon. Since frozen raspberries are ideal for this recipe, it can be prepared at any time of the year.

Thaw the fruit if frozen. Place in a liquidizer or food processor add the Sugar Syrup Sauce Base and vinegar and purée until smooth.

Press through a sieve to remove the seeds, then add the oil and freshly ground black pepper.

Makes about 600 ml/1 pint

Croque-monsieur of Goat's Cheese with Orange Vinaigrette

A delicious summer starter or luncheon dish. Substitute brandy or Cointreau for the pear liqueur, if you wish.

Cut rounds from the slices of bread, using a biscuit cutter. Heat the oil in a pan and fry the bread until crisp and golden. Drain well.

Turn the cutter over and fill it with cheese to a depth of about 1.5 cm/¾ inch. Lift off the cutter and place the cheese on the rounds of toast. Place under a grill until the cheese begins to melt.

Serve on individual starter plates garnished with frisé and chopped fresh chives. Scatter over the orange zest and drizzle the Orange Vinaigrette over, or pour it around.

Serves 6

6 slices bread

1 tablespoon groundnut oil

6 slices goat's cheese, rinds removed

To serve:
salad leaves, such as frisée

2 tablespoons chopped fresh chives

grated zest of ½ orange

Orange Vinaigrette (see previous page)

Grilled Salmon with Hot Orange Vinaigrette

My cousin, who lives in California, produced this delicious salmon recipe during my last visit there.

Brush the salmon with groundnut oil and char-grill on a barbecue or ridged frying pan (about 2 minutes each side). Half way through the cooking time, turn the fish 45° so the grill marks will produce an interesting cross-hatched effect. Repeat on the other sides of the fish.

Just before serving, heat the Orange Vinaigrette in a small pan, place the salmon cutlets or fillets on heated dinner plates, and drizzle the hot vinaigrette over. Garnish with pine nuts or flaked almonds, flakes of sea salt, cracked black pepper and sprigs of lambs' lettuce. I couldn't resist adding little boiled new potatoes – waxy yellow ones or pretty pink ones, such as pink fir apples.

Serves 6

6 salmon cutlets or tail fillets, about 250–375 g/8–12 oz each

1 tablespoon groundnut oil

Orange Vinaigrette (see previous page)

To garnish:
pine nuts or flaked almonds, toasted

flakes of sea salt

cracked black pepper

lambs' lettuce

Savoury Fruits with Sweet Mustard Vinaigrette

A most unusual starter, perfect for lunch or for dinners where you plan a very rich pudding. Choose fruits and vegetables in season, or select them with colour themes.

The one point I would make is that it is important to include some less sweet ingredients, especially grapefruit. The contrast is what 'makes' this dish.

This unusual vinaigrette is also an appropriate dressing for a green salad. Choose a selection of leaves – soft ones such as rocket, lettuce and lambs' lettuce, bitter ones such as radicchio or endive, and peppery ones such as tiny nasturtium leaves and watercress. Smoked meats, especially good-quality French smoked chicken or turkey, may also be added.

Place the vinegar and mustard in a liquidizer or food processor and blend until thoroughly mixed. Blend in the Sugar Syrup Sauce Base, then add the oil, slowly, a little at a time, to make an emulsion.

Cut the melon in half, deseed and remove the flesh with a melon-baller, or cut into slices. Halve and deseed the tomatoes and slice into wedges or cubes. Halve and slice the cucumber. Peel and segment the grapefruit and cut the grapes in half. Halve the avocado and remove the stone, then peel and slice the flesh.

Arrange the fruits and vegetables on a salad plate, then pour the dressing over at the last moment – or serve it separately in a small bowl or sauceboat.

Serves 6

4 tablespoons white wine vinegar

25 g/4 oz Dijon mustard

150 ml/¼ pint Sugar Syrup Sauce Base

450 ml/¾ pint oil, (e.g. groundnut, grapeseed or sunflower)

A selection of fruits and vegetables which could include: **Charentais or canteloupe melon, plum tomatoes, cucumber, grapefruit, kiwifruit, seedless green grapes, mouli, radish and avocado**

sprigs of mint, to garnish

Alternatively:
SWEET SALAD WITH LEAVES AND FLOWERS
Instead of the fruits, substitute a selection of leaves and flowers, then proceed as in the main recipe. I would use rocket, lambs' lettuce and watercress, with violets, rose petals and the leaves and flowers of nasturtiums. Aim for good colour combinations.

Onion Confit for Game Terrine

600 ml/1 pint red wine

150 ml/¼ pint red wine vinegar

425 g/14 oz onions, sliced

600 ml/1 pint water

50 g/2 oz butter

75 ml/3 fl oz Sugar Syrup Sauce Base

salt and freshly ground black pepper

This makes a good, contrasting side sauce for a game or pork terrine. Try adding a teaspoon of a scented eau-de-vie such as Poire William or kirsch as a variation.

Bring the wine and vinegar to the boil, add the onions and simmer gently until the liquid has disappeared. Add the water and reduce again to ensure that the onions are thoroughly cooked.

When the liquid base has once again reduced to a syrup, add the butter, Sugar Syrup Sauce Base and seasoning. Cook to a mush, taste and adjust the acidity with more vinegar if it seems necessary.

Serves 6

Glazed Onions

300 ml/½ pint Sugar Syrup Sauce Base

50 ml/2 fl oz red wine

150 ml/¼ pint red wine vinegar

150 ml/¼ pint water

500 g/1 lb onions

75 g/3 oz butter

Delicious with various chicken and meat dishes with red wine sauces, such as Coq au Vin on page 112, or the Barbary Duck Breasts with Creamed Celeriac on page 114. Slightly piquant, they should be macerated for several hours to achieve their full flavour. Use onion sets, silverskins, or just very small onions.

Pour the Sugar Syrup Sauce Base into a heavy-based pan, bring to the boil and reduce to a light caramel. Pour in the wine and vinegar, bring to the boil again and reduce until syrupy. Add the water and bring to the boil, making sure all the caramel has dissolved.

Meanwhile, plunge the onions into boiling water for 5 minutes. Drain and cool. Taking each onion in turn, cut off the base and squeeze the onion out of the root end. Heat the butter in a small pan and brown the onions gently, disturbing them as little as possible and keeping them covered until they are almost cooked (about 5 minutes).

Pour the sauce over the onions and simmer until tender. Leave in the sauce until needed, then return to boiling point, drain and serve.

Serves 6

Pork and Pasta in Hot Tomato Sauce

This is a delicious pork recipe – perfect teamed with pasta such as spaghetti or fettuccine. The spicy tomato sauce can also be served without meat for vegetarians. You could also substitute harissa instead of the chilli paste.

Heat the oil and butter in a pan, add the onion and fry gently until softened but not coloured. Add the tomatoes, herbs, Sugar Syrup Sauce Base, garlic and vinegar. Bring to the boil and simmer gently until the mixture is quite thick.

Place in a liquidizer or food processor, purée, then strain out the skin and pips. Taste and adjust the seasoning, then add the chilli paste or harissa, to taste.

Heat a non-stick pan, add the seasoned pork fillets and cook gently until lightly browned. Add the tomato mixture and continue cooking, basting the pork fillets from time to time, keeping them well coated with sauce.

Place the pork fillets on heated dinner plates and spoon over the sauce. Grate the Parmesan, sprinkle over the pasta, and serve.

Serves 6

50 ml/2 fl oz olive oil

50 g/2 oz butter

1 onion, chopped

1 kg/2 lb tomatoes, sliced

½ teaspoon dried thyme

½ teaspoon dried oregano

25 ml/1 fl oz
Sugar Syrup Sauce Base

1 clove of garlic, crushed

1 tablespoon white wine vinegar

chilli paste or harissa, to taste

2 large pork fillets, sliced

75 g/3 oz Parmesan cheese

375 g/12 oz pasta, cooked

salt and pepper

Hot Cumberland Sauce

I always use fresh redcurrants, but you could use frozen fruit – or even redcurrant jelly. Delicious when hot; thicker when cold.

Place the orange zest, Sugar Syrup Sauce Base and fruit in a non-metal or stainless steel pan and simmer for 50 minutes. Strain, then add the ginger, port and mustard. Return to the pan and simmer again until the whole is reduced to 350 ml/12 fl oz.

Alternatively, melt redcurrant jelly with the port. Add all the other ingredients except the Sugar Syrup Sauce Base. Boil until it becomes syrupy, but do not singe or brown the jelly by overheating.

Makes 350 ml/12 fl oz

grated zest of 1 orange

750 ml/1¼ pints
Sugar Syrup Sauce Base

1 kg/2 lb redcurrants

1 tablespoon puréed stem ginger

150 ml/¼ pint port

1 tablespoon Dijon mustard

Veal Kidneys in a Golden Piquant Sauce

150 ml/¼ pint
Sugar Syrup Sauce Base

125 ml/4 fl oz red wine vinegar

150 ml/¼ pint water

1 carrot, scraped into
long thin strips with a lemon
zester, or cut into julienne

2 teaspoons Dijon mustard

1 teaspoon arrowroot
or cornflour

150 ml/¼ pint
chicken or veal stock

36 thin slices of veal kidney
(about 175 g/6 oz per person)

about 125 g/4 oz clarified
butter, (see below)

salt and freshly
ground black pepper

Note:

CLARIFIED BUTTER
To clarify the butter, heat it
in a saucepan, pour off the
clear portion and discard the
solids. Concentrated butter,
available in supermarkets,
is an alternative. Ghee, used
in Indian cooking, is also a
type of clarified butter.

This sauce is a beautiful limpid golden colour, and its sweet-sour flavour has a special appeal for the British palate. Don't attempt this recipe, however, unless you have some rich, good-quality jellied stock. It certainly won't work using a stock cube!

The only alternative to veal kidney – which can be difficult to get – is to use young, full, pale, lambs' kidneys, very thinly sliced into piccata-like rounds.

Personally I do not like to wash kidneys, because the water boils during cooking and destroys the meat texture. There is no need as long as they are very fresh, and you remove the white centre cores. If you do, make sure you dry them well.

Place the Sugar Syrup Sauce Base in a saucepan and simmer gently until it becomes a rich caramel colour.

Turn off the heat and immediately pour all the vinegar in at once and boil up furiously. Do not be tempted to stir the mixture or it will become a thick lump of sugar and take a long time to dissolve.

When the liquid stops bubbling, add the water and carrot strips and simmer until all the sugar is dissolved, leaving about 150 ml/¼ pint. Remove the carrot strips as soon as they are cooked.

Mix the mustard and arrowroot together, then mix with the cold stock and stir into the pan. Add salt and pepper to taste and simmer until the sauce has thickened.

Remove all fat and membrane from the kidneys and slice them into thin rounds. Season with salt and freshly ground black pepper. Heat the clarified butter in a non-stick pan until very hot. Add the kidneys in batches and fry them quickly for just a few seconds on each side. Remove and drain on kitchen paper. Set aside in a warm place.

Place the slices on heated starter plates and spoon the sauce around. Garnish with the carrot strips and serve immediately.

Serves 6

Caramel Sauce for Poached Pears or Ice-cream

150 ml/¼ pint
Sugar Syrup Sauce Base

150 ml/¼ pint water

150 ml/¼ pint double
or whipping cream

A very sweet, almost fudgy, sauce which I like best with poached pears. To make a creamier, thicker sauce, add another 300 ml/½ pint cream and boil it down to the desired thickness. Remember that, as the sauce cools it becomes thicker. If too thick, thin out with water.

Boil the Sugar Syrup Sauce Base until caramelized. Remove from the heat to a heatproof surface. Pour on all the water in one go, taking your hand away very quickly to avoid a steam burn. This will usually dissolve all the caramel. If not, return to the heat and simmer until completely melted.

Pour on the cream and simmer for 1 minute, then serve hot or cold.
Serves 6

Caramel Custard Ice

300 ml/½ pint
Sugar Syrup Sauce Base

150 ml/¼ pint water

450 ml/¾ pint milk

5 eggs

50 g/2 oz sugar

200 ml/7 fl oz crème fraîche

This is a variation of the English custard ice which used to be made by stirring the custard in a container over a salt and ice mixture until it froze. Although richer, this still makes a refreshing change from a cream ice. For an even smoother and more indulgent ice, use 10 egg yolks instead of 5 whole eggs.

Pour the Sugar Syrup Base into a large heavy pan, and boil until caramelized to a mahogany colour. Add the water and boil furiously until the sugar dissolves, adding more water if necessary. Reduce until slightly syrupy, then add the milk and return to the boil.

Place the eggs and sugar in a liquidizer or food processor and mix well. Without stopping the motor, pour the caramel-flavoured milk on to the eggs, then return the mixture to the rinsed saucepan.

Heat almost to boiling point, but do not allow to curdle. If it begins to curdle, pour immediately into the blender and whizz until smooth.

Finally, pour it through a sieve into a bowl, then cool. When cold, stir in the crème fraîche and freeze the mixture in a sorbetière, or according to the method on page 171.
Serves 6

Mascarpone Ice-cream with a Passionfruit Coulis

The true flavour of this cooked fruit sauce emerges only when cooled. It is also delicious used hot (and thus more liquid) over ice-cream. The colour is a beautiful, limpid jewel-like crimson-purple, thanks to the passionfruit shells (without the shells, the sauce is golden).

Freeze the ice-cream in a long, narrow loaf tin, so it can be either cut into slices or scooped into balls.

Place all the ice-cream ingredients in a liquidizer or food processor, purée until smooth. Pour into a long, narrow container and freeze.

To make the sauce, cut the passionfruit in half and scrape the insides into a large stainless steel pan. Add the empty shells.

Pour in the Sugar Syrup Sauce Base and add enough water to cover. Bring to the boil and simmer for 10 minutes. Using a potato masher, press down and squash the shells to extract all possible flavour. Simmer for a further 2 minutes then strain the juice through a sieve, using the back of a spoon to squeeze through all the jelly from around the seeds and any colour from the shells. Return the juice to the pan, bring to the boil and reduce to approximately 300 ml/½ pint. Cool.

To serve, cut 1–2 slices of ice-cream, depending on appetite, pour the passionfruit sauce around, and decorate with a few whole seeds.

Serves 6

For the mascarpone ice-cream:
265 g/8½ oz mascarpone

3 egg yolks

4 tablespoons sugar

grated zest of ½ orange

For the passionfruit coulis:
6 passionfruit

150 ml/¼ pint
Sugar Syrup Sauce Base

water to cover

whole passionfruit seeds, to decorate

Pineapple Sauce

Bliss with ice-cream – and also as a hot sauce over a sponge pudding, or mixed with a whipped egg white and frozen into a sorbet.

Place the pineapple in a saucepan, add the Sugar Syrup Sauce Base, bring to the boil and simmer for 20 minutes. Cool, then add the brandy to cut the sweetness. Leave for 24 hours before use.

You can use lemon juice instead of brandy but it has a different effect – almost sweet and sour.

Serves 6

1 kg/2 lb whole pineapple, peeled and chopped or 500 g/1 lb pineapple flesh, chopped

600 ml/1 pint
Sugar Syrup Sauce Base

50 ml/2 fl oz brandy

169

Pear Cream Ice

275 g/9 oz no-need-to-soak
dried pears

250 ml/8 fl oz
Sugar Syrup Sauce Base

zest and juice of 1 lemon

300 ml/½ pint water

150 ml/¼ pint Egg Sauce Base
(see page 14)

150 ml/¼ pint double cream

50 ml/2 fl oz *eau-de-vie de poire*
(optional)

A rich, delicate ice-cream. Since pears are not a very acid fruit, any pungency has to be added in the form of lemon juice.

Poire William or another eau-de-vie will give an extra zing to the pear taste, but you could substitute Calvados if you wished.

Place the pears, Sugar Syrup Sauce Base, lemon zest and juice, water and Egg Sauce Base in a liquidizer or food processor and purée until smooth. Whip the cream, fold into the mixture and chill until firm, then liquidize again, adding the *eau-de-vie*, if using, and a little more lemon juice to sharpen the taste if necessary. Freeze according to the directions on page 173.

Remove from the freezer 15 minutes before serving. To serve, pile into glasses and serve with a Cold Caramel Sauce (see page 168).
Serves 6

Brandied Kumquats

150 g/5 oz fresh kumquats

150 ml/¼ pint water

300 ml/½ pint
Sugar Syrup Sauce Base

50 ml/2 fl oz brandy

This is a very versatile recipe. It appears as part of the delicious White Chocolate Mousse with Three Chocolate Sauces on page 185 – because citrus fruits, especially oranges and kumquats, have a special affinity with chocolate.

Kumquats, with their rather sharp flavour, also complement rich or particularly flavourful meats, such as game, pork, goose, and duck, such as Duck Breasts in Orange Burgundy Sauce on page 117.

Slice the kumquats in half, or cut in a dog-tooth pattern around the middle. Place in a non-metal or stainless steel saucepan, pour in the water, bring to the boil and simmer for 10 minutes.

Add the Sugar Syrup Sauce Base, bring to the boil and add the fruit and simmer gently for a further 10 minutes, allow to cool, then add the brandy and serve.
Serves 6

Melon Sorbet

Melons vary in flavour from insipid to pungent, and the better the melon, the better the sorbet. Because melons hold so much water, the Sauce Base has to hold less and the easiest way to achieve this is to add more sugar. Cool the syrup before you pour it over the melon or you'll cook the fruit and spoil the flavour.

Heat the Sugar Syrup Sauce Base in a saucepan, add the extra sugar and dissolve. Allow to cool but not chill (it will be rather treacly).

Place the melon flesh, lemon juice and syrup in a liquidizer or food processor and purée. Add more lemon juice as necessary.

Add the Pernod drop by drop to point up the flavour. Freeze. When very firm, put in a blender and purée to whiten it. A raw egg white may be added to stabilize the mixture and soften the taste.

Freeze, but soften in the refrigerator for 15 minutes before serving.
Serves 6

150 ml/¼ pint
Sugar Syrup Sauce Base

175 g/6 oz granulated sugar

1 large melon

juice of 2 lemons
(about 6 tablespoons)

1 teaspoon Pernod

1 egg white (optional)

Grapefruit Sorbet

This sorbet packs quite a punch and cleans the palate – delicious when combined with other sorbets as in the illustration overleaf. The secret is to cook the zest but not the flesh or juice. This is generally true of all citrus sorbets, as most of the flavour is in the outer skin.

Bring the Sugar Syrup Sauce Base to the boil, add the zest from all the fruit and simmer for 10 minutes.

Cut the fruit in half, squeeze out the juice and pull out the flesh. Leave it to drain in a sieve set over a bowl. Discard the white pith. Put the flesh in the pan, and turn off the heat.

Cool, then press the juice through the sieve and discard the fibre. Add the fruit juices and adjust the sugar level with a little extra if needed. Chill in a freezer until just set hard.

Place the mixture in a blender and break it down quickly to whiten it. At this point you can add a raw egg white to stabilize the mixture further and soften the taste. Freeze again, but remove 15 minutes before serving and leave it in the refrigerator to soften.
Serves 6

300 ml/½ pint
Sugar Syrup Sauce Base

4 grapefruit

2 lemons

1 egg white (optional)

Alternatively:
GINGER SORBET
Purée a jar of stem ginger together with its syrup. Proceed as in the main recipe and add a tablespoon (or more according to taste) of the ginger purée to the cooled mixture before freezing.

Nectarine Sorbet

Because the fruit in this recipe is not cooked at all, it must be of the very best quality – ripe, perfectly sound and ready to eat. If they are not yet ready, keep them for a few days to let the flavour develop. Reject any spoiled fruit.

The skin gives colour and depth of flavour. The lemon juice must be added to the fruit before being puréed, otherwise you get a nasty brown mush that looks revolting. The pretty red flecks of skin are very much part of the attraction of this sorbet, so don't strain out.

Cut the nectarines in half and remove the stones. Pour the lemon juice into a stainless steel or non-metal bowl, then add the nectarine flesh, tossing it in the juice, to prevent discoloration.

Place the fruit and juice in a liquidizer or food processor, then add the cold Sugar Syrup Sauce Base.

Freeze the sorbet in a sorbetière if you have one. Otherwise chill in the freezer until firm. Scrape the mixture into a liquidizer or food processor and purée quickly to whiten the mixture. Freeze again until firm. To serve, remove 15 minutes before serving and leave in the refrigerator to soften.

Serves 6

6 ripe nectarines

juice of about 3 lemons

**300 ml/½ pint
Sugar Syrup Sauce Base**

Alternatively:
GREEN APPLE SORBET
Make in the same way, substituting a large, ripe Bramley apple, weighing about 250 g/8 oz, together with 100 ml/3½ fl oz lemon juice, 450 ml/¾ pint Sugar Syrup Sauce Base. Add 1 beaten egg white before freezing as in the main recipe.

*Illustrated left:
White Grapefruit Sorbet, pink Nectarine Sorbet and pale orange Melon Sorbet. Serve a selection of flavours, or just one. Decorate each serving with sprigs of mint, if liked.*

Passionfruit Soufflé

2 egg, separated

6 tablespoons passionfruit coulis (see recipe page 169) made with Sugar Syrup Sauce Base

50 g/2 oz granulated sugar

butter, for greasing

This is a really easy, conversation-stopping dessert. So long as you have some Passionfruit Coulis (see page 169) in your refrigerator it can be made at short notice. As with most meringue dishes you need a sweet tooth to enjoy it – not a rare attribute, I found, especially at the Horn of Plenty.

Ring the changes by substituting different fruits – especially the more unusual ones – for a more spectacular effect. Try, for instance, substituting the flesh of a custard apple (cherimoya), poached for a few minutes with 2 tablespoons of sugar and 1 tablespoon lemon juice. Measure out 6 tablespoons of the resulting purée and proceed as in the main recipe.

Other interesting variations include persimmon, pomegranate, plum or lime and ginger. Prepare the pomegranate pulp in the same way as the passionfruit coulis

Whisk the egg yolks until thick and pale. Add the passionfruit syrup and whisk over heat until thickened.

In a separate bowl whisk the egg whites until very stiff, and add the sugar, half at a time. Fold into the egg yolk mixture.

Take 6 small soufflé dishes and butter them well. Fill them three-quarters full with the mixture and cook in a preheated oven at 200–220°C (400–425°F) Gas Mark 6–7 for 7 minutes until well risen, then serve immediately.

Serves 6

Alternatively:

POMEGRANATE SOUFFLÉ

Make pomegranate syrup in the same way as Passionfruit Coulis on page 169 – using 6 small pomegranates instead of the passionfruit. Do not include the bitter white pith or the shells. Make the soufflés as described in the main recipe. You could also substitute 1 tablespoon of Grenadine for the pomegranate syrup.

PLUM SOUFFLÉ

Use the plum syrup from the Plum Bavarois recipe on the opposite page instead of the passionfruit syrup, and proceed as in the main recipe.

Apple Charlotte

A favourite childhood recipe – frying the bread first ensures it stays crunchy. The apple purée must be very thick or the excess liquid will make the pudding collapse when you turn it out.

Brown the Sugar Syrup Sauce Base lightly, add the water and dissolve the sugar again in the water. Cook the apple in the mixture until soft, then cook further in a microwave or non-stick pan until it dries out.

Line a soufflé dish or deep ovenproof pie dish with slices of bread cut to size, each one slightly overlapping its neighbour, with extra for the top. Brown the slices in the butter on one side only and replace them in the dish, brown side out, with no gaps in between. Spoon in the hot purée, add extra slices to the top and bake in a preheated oven at 230°C (450°F) Gas Mark 8 for 40 minutes. Turn out the charlotte (while crossing your fingers), and serve with egg custard.

Serves 6

**300 ml/½ pint
Sugar Syrup Sauce Base**

150 ml/¼ pint water

**1.5 kg/3 lb Bramley cooking
apples, peeled, cored and sliced**

**1 loaf good white bread,
sliced thickly**

250 g/8 oz butter, for frying

Oranges in Brandy

This is an old favourite of my sous-chef Glyn Green, much enjoyed at the Horn, and easy to make this way.

Using a zester, remove the zest from the oranges in long matchstick strips. Boil the Sugar Syrup Sauce Base to a dark caramel colour. Add the water, spices and orange zest, bring to the boil and reduce to about 200 ml/7 fl oz. Add the brandy and Grand Marnier.

Remove all the pith from the oranges, slice them in rounds and arrange them in a heatproof glass dish. Pour over the Sugar Syrup Sauce Base and allow to cool without disturbing the oranges.

Alternatively, if you prefer to serve whole oranges, add them before the liqueurs with a further 150 ml/¼ pint water to cover. Add the brandy and Grand Marnier.

Pick out the cinnamon, cloves and mace, then chill. Serve with a crunchy biscuit such as brandy snaps.

Serves 6

6 oranges

**300 ml/½ pint
Sugar Syrup Sauce Base**

300 ml/½ pint water

8 cloves

**5 cm/2 inches piece
of cinnamon stick**

1 small piece of whole mace

2 tablespoons brandy

2 tablespoons Grand Marnier

Plum Bavarois with Red Wine and Angelica Sauce

12 plums

300 ml/½ pint
Sugar Syrup Sauce Base

450 ml/¾ pint milk

6 egg yolks

175 g/6 oz sugar

1 tablespoon cornflour

4 sheets gelatine, soaked in
cold water or 1 packet
granules, dissolved

150 ml/¼ pint whipped cream

Vieille Prune eau-de-vie,
or brandy, to taste

For the sauce:

250 ml/8 fl oz red wine

150 ml/¼ pint
Sugar Syrup Sauce Base

125 g/4 oz young, fresh
angelica, cut into small pieces

To decorate:
angelica leaves

plum slices

I discovered this way of producing a red wine sauce when I was instructing a student from South Africa. She said they had plenty of red wine and sugar available, but no soft fruits such as raspberries to make fruit sauces. This was the solution – the angelica gives the sauce a delicate, scented whisper of flavour.

I have angelica in my garden. It is very easy to grow and makes a tall, handsome plant with huge balls of flowers in the summer. Use the small fresh stems for this recipe – easy, because angelica is one of those 'cut-and-come-again' plants. Rose or lemon scented geranium leaves could be substituted.

If you can get leaf gelatine, it is much easier to work with. Granules should be dissolved in water separately, then added in the same way as the leaves.

To make the sauce, bring all the ingredients to the boil and reduce to approximately 175 ml/6 fl oz. Strain.

To make the bavarois, cut the plums in half and remove the stones. Place the fruit in a large saucepan and pour over the Sugar Syrup Sauce Base. Simmer the fruit for approximately 20 minutes until it is well cooked and soft. Strain the fruit and keep the syrup for another use such as plum soufflé, sorbet or to pour over ice-cream. Purée the plums in a liquidizer or food processor.

To make the custard, first bring the milk to the boil. Mix the egg yolks, sugar and cornflour in a bowl, then – mixing all the time – pour in the hot milk. When this is smooth, pour it back into the pan and bring it to just short of boiling point.

Add the gelatine and strain into a clean bowl.

Mix in the plum purée and allow to cool but not set. Fold in the whipped cream, add the *eau-de-vie* or brandy, and fill 6 individual moulds with the mixture. Turn out the bavarois on to small plates, and serve with the sauce poured around, and decorated with slices of plum and small pieces of angelica leaf.

Serves 6

Iced Mousse Cake with Apricot Custard

This Apricot Custard is very versatile – and delicious enough to serve on its own as a cold dessert if you make it with a larger quantity of the Sugar Syrup Sauce Base. Serve it in tall glasses with pieces of buttery shortbread.

To make the Apricot Custard, place the apricots in a liquidizer or food processor, add the Sugar Syrup Sauce Base and purée until smooth. Pour into a saucepan and heat until almost boiling. Return the mixture to the liquidizer or food processor, add the Egg Sauce Base, and blend until thoroughly mixed. Cool before serving.

To make the Iced Mousse Cake, line a long terrine mould, first with clingfilm and then with two-thirds of the slices of Madeira cake. Mix the brandy and liqueurs together and pour over about two-thirds of the mixture. Place the reserved slices of cake in a separate bowl and pour over the remaining liqueur mixture.

Melt the chocolate in a bowl over boiling water. Toast the hazelnut chips until lightly brown and mix with the glacé fruits.

Break up the meringues into sugar-lump-sized pieces. Whip the cream until stiff and add the nuts, glacé fruit and meringues, followed by the melted chocolate.

In a separate bowl, whip the egg whites until firm. Slowly whisk in the icing sugar until very thick. Fold into the chocolate mixture.

Spoon the mixture into the cake-lined terrine and top with the remaining liqueur-soaked slices of cake. Press down gently and place a weight on top.

Freeze until firm and serve with Apricot Custard.

Serves 6

500 g/1 lb Madeira cake, sliced

75 ml/3 fl oz brandy

50 ml/2 fl oz Cointreau

50 ml/2 fl oz Galliano

50 g/2 oz Menier or other good-quality chocolate

50 g/2 oz hazelnut chips

50 g/2 oz glacé fruits, chopped

2 meringues (see page 183)

300 ml/½ pint whipping cream

3 egg whites

75 g/3 oz icing sugar

For the apricot custard:
125 g/4 oz no-need-to-soak dried apricots

250 ml/8 fl oz Sugar Syrup Sauce Base

150 ml/¼ pint Egg Sauce Base (see page 14)

Alternatively:
APRICOT PARFAIT
Purée the apricots with a further 150 ml/¼ pint of Sugar Syrup Sauce Base. Serve in tall glasses with pieces of shortbread and slices of fresh apricot.

Little Fruit Tarts with Passionfruit Coulis

125 g/4 oz plain flour

1 teaspoon sugar

150 g/5 oz butter,
cut into pieces

4 tablespoons iced water

salt

1 beaten egg yolk, to glaze

For the crème pâtissière:
6 egg yolks

125 g/4 oz sugar

40 g/1½ oz plain flour

450 ml/¾ pint milk

vanilla or *eau-de-vie*, to taste

For the fruit filling:
500 g/1 lb mixed fresh fruits,
such as strawberries,
raspberries, blueberries, red
or white currants, kiwifrui,
sugar-poached tamarillos,
or starfruit (carambola)

For the glaze:
3 tablespoons redcurrant jelly,
simmered for 2 minutes
with 1 tablespoon water

To serve:
Passionfruit Coulis (page 169)

whipped cream (optional)

These tarts are some of the great classics French cuisine. Most French people would buy them from the pâtisserie – and they would taste marvellous. But they are incredibly easy to make yourself, and make a terrific impression at a dinner party.

Use a mixture of fruits in season and serve with a fruit sauce, such as the Passionfruit Coulis shown here, and extra whipped cream for people like my husband – who simply cannot resist 'staving off the fatal day' as he terms it.

To make the pastry, mix the flour, salt and sugar together then, with your fingertips, rub in the butter until the mixture resembles fine breadcrumbs. Add the water and gather everything together to form a ball, working the mixture as little as possible. Wrap in clingfilm and chill for at least 2 hours.

Roll out and line six 10 cm/4 inch tart tins, or 1 large one, press the pastry against the side and cut the top flush with the tin. Bake blind (see note, page 181) in a preheated oven at 200°C (400°F) Gas Mark 6 for about 10 minutes for the small tins or 20–25 minutes for the large. Remove the paper and beans or foil and bake for 3–5 minutes more to dry out the pastry. Remove from the oven, brush with the beaten egg yolk, return to the oven for 1 minute, then remove and leave to cool.

To make the crème pâtissière, place the egg yolks, sugar and flour in a liquidizer or food processor and blend until smooth. Heat the milk to boiling point. Remove from the heat and pour on to the mixture, with the motor running. Pour into a clean pan, bring to the boil and beat well so it cooks evenly. It will thicken, but continue boiling until the flour is thoroughly cooked and smooth (about 2 minutes). Remove from the heat, add the vanilla or *eau-de-vie*, pour into the pastry cases, and leave to set.

To assemble, place the cooled pastry case or cases on serving plates, and spread the cold crème pâtissière in the base or bases. Arrange the fruit on top and brush with the glaze. Set aside to cool completely, then serve with Passionfruit Coulis and whipped cream if using.
Serves 6

Starfruit and Almond Tarts

375 g/12 oz sweet shortcrust pastry (see page 178)

3 starfruit

a little water

450 ml/¾ pint Sugar Syrup Sauce Base

3 tablespoons Pernod

150 ml/¼ pint double cream

For the frangipane filling:
125 g/4 oz unsalted butter

125 g/4 oz ground almonds

125 g/4 oz caster sugar

50 g/2 oz plain flour

4 small eggs (size 4)

The Starfruit, or Carambola, looks so attractive that one can almost forgive its singular lack of flavour.

The remedy is to soak it overnight in a strong flavour. Sugar and Pernod taste wonderful together and not too aniseedy. This recipe should be started the day before so the Pernod can penetrate the fruit.

Make the pastry as described in the recipe for Little Fruit Tarts on page 178, roll it out as thinly as possible, then line 6 individual tartlet cases, 10 cm/4 inches in diameter. Chill, then bake blind (see opposite) in a preheated oven at 200°C (400°F) Gas Mark 6 for 10 minutes. Remove the beans and foil, return to the oven for 5 minutes to dry out and set aside to cool.

Slice the starfruit into rings, place in a pan with water to cover, bring to the boil and simmer for 10 minutes. Drain, add the Sugar Syrup Sauce Base, bring to the boil and simmer for 30 minutes more, topping up with a little water now and again to prevent the sugar from becoming too hot and caramelizing.

Using a slotted spoon, lift the starfruit into a clean bowl, retaining the syrup. Pour the Pernod over the fruit so it is thoroughly coated. Leave overnight to macerate in the refrigerator.

To make the filling, cream the butter in a mixer, then add the dry ingredients followed by the eggs. Beat well to incorporate some air to lighten the mixture.

Spoon the mixture into the tartlet cases and cook in a preheated oven at 180°C (350°F) Gas Mark 4 for about 10 minutes. Place the starfruit rings on top, pressing them gently into the filling. Reduce the oven temperature to 150°C (300°F) Gas Mark 2 for about 15 minutes to finish cooking. Make sure the filling has set completely before removing the tarts from the oven.

To make the sauce, simmer the syrup and cream together and adding Pernod from the maceration, reducing if necessary. Pour around the tartlets, and serve.

Serves 6

Hot Tarts with Coffee Sauce

You will need only a little meringue for this dish – the rest of the mixture can be kept refrigerated until needed or beaten into pastry cream, made into butter cream or meringues which must be baked until dry in the usual way. Since the egg whites are already half cooked, the meringues take far less time than the Swiss method of just beating sugar and egg whites together.

Make 6 individual tart bases using the recipe on page 178. Bake blind (see below right) in a preheated oven at 200°C (400°F) Gas Mark 6 for 10 minutes, remove the paper and beans or foil, return to the oven for 5 minutes to dry out, then remove from the oven and set aside to cool.

To make the filling, pour the milk into a non-stick pan and bring it almost to boiling point. Mix the egg yolks and flour in a liquidizer or food processor. With the machine still running, pour in the hot milk until the egg mixture is thoroughly dissolved.

Return the mixture to the rinsed milk pan. Bring to the boil and cook gently for 2 minutes, stirring constantly, to prevent the mixture from sticking to the base and browning. Add the chosen flavouring and fold in the Italian meringue.

Fill the tarts with the mixture and bake in a preheated oven at 120°C (300°F) Gas Mark 2 for about 30 minutes until set.

To make the sauce, simply mix all the ingredients together and serve separately in a sauceboat. Alternatively, serve with any fruit coulis, such as Passionfruit Coulis or Pineapple Sauce on page 169, or Rum Cream, using the recipe for Coffee Sauce, substituting rum for coffee.

Serves 6

6 sweet shortcrust tart bases, (see page 178)

For the filling:
450 ml/¾ pint milk

6 egg yolks

40g/1½ oz flour

vanilla, or 3 tablespoons Kirsch or other *eau-de-vie*, to taste

125 g/4 oz Italian meringue made with Sugar Sauce Base, (see page 183)

salt

For the coffee sauce:
Cream Sauce Base made from 350 ml/12 fl oz whipping cream (see page 52)

25 ml/1 fl oz very strong espresso coffee (or to taste)

125 ml/4 fl oz Sugar Syrup Sauce Base, made from 75 g/3 oz sugar and 75 ml/3 fl oz water

Note:
BAKING BLIND
To bake 'blind', prick the dough and line the tin with non-stick paper or foil, and fill with beans, stones or rice to weigh it down. Remove and dry out in the oven for 5 minutes before proceeding with the recipe.

Eclairs with Fondant Topping

150 g/5 oz butter

300 ml/½ pint water

at least 175 g/6 oz
plain flour (be generous)

5 eggs

about ½ teaspoon salt

300 ml/½ pint whipping cream,
whipped with 1 teaspoon icing
sugar, to decorate

For the fondant topping:
300 ml/½ pint
Sugar Syrup Sauce Base

50 g/2 oz dark plain
chocolate, broken into pieces

Making fondant is a most satisfying experience. It can be flavoured for variation with essences or colours, such as strawberry, lemon or coffee, instead of chocolate – but chocolate wins every time!

Freshly cooked éclairs are crisp and delicious, so it's worthwhile knowing that the mixture can be made, piped in advance, and deep-frozen. The cooking can be done from frozen, adding five minutes to the oven times. You'll find that this is very much better than the usual method of storing in an airtight tin.

To make the fondant, boil the Sugar Syrup Sauce Base at about 5°C/2°F higher than boiling point (100°C/212°F). Pour it out on to a cold surface and allow to cool a little (about 10 seconds).

Work the mixture vigorously with 2 forks, starting from the edges and working towards the centre, picking up all the sugar until it turns white. Knead it together with your hands – it is now fondant.

Melt the chocolate in a double boiler, then add the fondant and water – ½ teaspoon at a time – until a smooth, slightly runny texture results. Keep warm.

To make the choux pastry for the éclairs, place the butter, water and salt in a pan and heat gently until the butter melts, then bring to the boil. Tip all the flour in at once, stir vigorously and cook the mixture until it forms a single slippery ball. Quickly place this in a food processor, so as not to lose too much heat, and add the eggs, one at a time, allowing each egg to mix in thoroughly before adding the next.

Spoon the mixture into a piping bag fitted with a plain nozzle, and pipe into balls or lengths according to whether you want puffs or éclairs, and leaving plenty of room between them for expansion. Bake in a preheated oven at 200°C (400°F) Gas Mark 6 for approximately 20 minutes. Slit each éclair to allow the steam to escape or make a round hole in the base of the puffs and dry them for 5 minutes longer in the oven. Remove any soggy mixture from the insides. Pipe in the whipped cream along the length of the éclairs or through the hole made in the base of the puffs. Finally dip the tops in chocolate fondant and cool, until the fondant is set. Eat as soon as possible.

Makes approximately 36

Chocolate Meringue Cake

Allow plenty of time to make this because there are several steps. The meringue sheets can be cooked in advance and kept in an airtight tin for a few days. When it is all assembled it can be well wrapped in foil and frozen, but will probably need redecorating when thawed.

To give you some idea of the size of this cake, I use the lid of a Le Crueset terrine as a template for the meringue rectangles.

Heat the Sugar Syrup Sauce Base further, until it reaches the 'hard ball' stage when it will solidify when dropped into cold water. Whisk the egg whites until very firm and, still beating vigorously, pour in the hot Sugar Syrup Sauce Base. Continue to beat until the mixture is thick and shiny.

With a pencil, mark 5 rectangles, 10 x 25 cm/4 x 10 inches on sheets of non-stick baking paper. Fill the outlines with half the meringue mix, keeping it as flat as possible. Place in a preheated oven to dry at 110°C (225°F) Gas Mark ¼. This should not take more than 1 hour, because the meringue will already have been half dried out.

To make the filling, place the coffee, chocolate and water in a pan over hot water and mix until smooth. Set aside to cool.

In a separate bowl, beat the butter until creamed, then add the cooled chocolate, mixing well. Add the other half of the meringue and beat it all together. Cover until ready to use.

Cool the meringue sheets and peel them off the paper as you put the cake together. It doesn't really matter if they break up a bit as they are going to be completely covered in chocolate, but make sure that the bottom one is whole and fix it to a board with a blob of filling. Using this as the base, spread over a layer of filling, followed by a sheet of meringue, and repeat until all the meringue is used, and finish with a layer of filling. Finally, spread this layer down the sides and all over the sheets, making the cake airtight, with no white meringue showing.

Set aside in a cool place – or in the refrigerator – to set, then use within 2 days, or wrap in foil and freeze. Thaw in the refrigerator for about 1 hour before use. Slice like a loaf of bread and serve with a good, dark, bitter chocolate sauce, as on page 185.

Serves 6

1.2 litres/2 pints
Sugar Syrup Sauce Base

10 egg whites

non-stick baking paper

For the filling:
6 tablespoons extra-strong espresso coffee

275 g/9 oz good-quality cooking chocolate, such as Menier, broken into pieces

3 tablespoons water

750 g/1½ lb unsalted butter

Note:
MERINGUE MAKING METHODS
The method described at left not only allows the mixture to become crunchy more quickly when it is dried out in the oven, but also may be kept in its soft state in an airtight container for about a week, in the refrigerator and used as required. It goes soggy after a while, and the sugar/meringue melts just like ordinary meringue.

White Chocolate Mousse, with Three Chocolate Sauces

The Three Chocolate Sauces are very simple – make the dark sauce first, and the two paler ones by adding more Cream Sauce Base. Stop when you reach the desired colour. Serve with Brandied Kumquats (recipe on page 170), which must be simmered in plain water to make sure they're tender before the Sugar Sauce Base is added. The brandy removes any cloying sweetness and gives a sophisticated zip to the finished sauce.

To make the mousse, first soak the gelatine leaves in cold water. Place the chocolate in a pan and, stirring constantly, add the water, sugar and Cointreau and heat very gently until the chocolate has melted. Squeeze excess water from the gelatine, then add to the chocolate mixture. Beat in the egg yolks and cool. Whip the cream to soft peaks and fold into the setting (but not solidified) mixture. Pour into 6 small brioche tins or mousse moulds, or 1 large mould, then chill.

To make the Three Chocolate Sauces, first make the darkest one. Mix the cocoa powder thoroughly with the oil in a small saucepan, then mix in the Sugar Syrup Sauce Base, a little at a time, to remove any lumps. Bring to the boil, cook until smooth, then set aside one-third of the mixture to cool.

To make the two paler sauces, first make the Cream Sauce Base. Pour the whipping cream into a non-stick pan, bring to the boil and reduce to a coating consistency, as in Step 2, page 52. Add about half the mixture to the remaining two-thirds of the chocolate sauce. Set aside one-half of the mixture. This is the second chocolate sauce.

To make the palest sauce, add the remaining Cream Sauce Base to the remaining mixture and stir well. Cool all three sauces.

To serve, turn the mousses out on to 6 small plates, and spoon the Three Chocolate Sauces, Brandied Kumquats and kumquat syrup beside. Alternatively, turn out the large mould on to a chilled serving plate, decorate with the kumquats and their syrup and serve with a single dark chocolate sauce in a separate sauceboat.

Serves 6

4 sheets gelatine or 1 packet granules soaked in water

300 g/10 oz white chocolate, broken into pieces

2 tablespoons water

1 tablespoon sugar

2 tablespoons Cointreau

3 egg yolks

600 ml/1 pint whipping cream

For the three chocolate sauces:
50 g/2 oz unsweetened cocoa powder

75 ml/3 fl oz grapeseed oil or groundnut oil

300 ml/½ pint Sugar Syrup Sauce Base

Cream Sauce Base, made from 300 ml/½ pint whipping cream (see page 52)

Brandied Kumquats, to serve (recipe on page 170)

Chocolate Grand Marnier Cake

250 g/8 oz good-quality cooking
chocolate, such as Menier

3 tablespoons Grand Marnier

300 ml/½ pint
Sugar Syrup Sauce Base

3 egg yolks

250 g/8 oz sugar

125 g/4 oz cornflour

4 egg whites

For the white chocolate spread:
300 g/10 oz good-quality
white chocolate

150 ml/¼ pint Egg Sauce Base
(see page 14)

65 g/2½ oz caster sugar

3 tablespoons Cointreau

sifted icing sugar, for dusting

Quite a squidgy cake – which can also be served as a pudding. In fact it's the ideal pudding to serve with clotted cream!

Use the White Chocolate Spread to make the filling for this recipe, and also for the Chocolate Biscuit Cake recipe opposite. Start with 450 ml/¾ pint Egg Sauce Base. Use one-third of that mixture for this recipe and the rest for the Brown Chocolate Spread.

It is important to use deep cake tins. Cool the cakes, still inside the tins, upside down on a rack for about 5 minutes. This keeps the cake properly risen and stops it collapsing. The tops of these cakes form a lovely, crunchy, meringue-like crust.

To make the White Chocolate Spread, break the white chocolate into a heatproof bowl and melt it gently over hot water.

Spoon the Egg Sauce Base into a separate bowl, then add the sugar, melted white chocolate and Cointreau and beat well. Thin out with water if necessary and use as a filling.

To make the cake, grease and line two deep 19 cm/7½ inch cake tins with non-stick paper. Break the chocolate into a heatproof bowl, add the Grand Marnier and melt over a pan of hot water, stirring.

Pour the Sugar Syrup Sauce Base into a bowl, add the egg yolks and half the sugar, and mix well. Mix in the chocolate mixture, then sift in the cornflour. Mix, then thin out with 3 tablespoons water.

In a separate bowl, whisk the egg whites until they form soft peaks, and beat in the remaining sugar, as for meringue (see page 183). Whisk until firm, then fold into the chocolate mix. Divide the mixture between the two deep cake tins.

Place in a preheated oven at 180°C (350°F) Gas Mark 4 for about 25 minutes. Remove from the oven and place upside down, still in the tins, on to wire racks and rest for 5 minutes.

Remove the tins, peel off the paper and allow to steam and cool before turning them over. Layer with the White Chocolate Spread filling, putting the crunchy 'meringue' tops of the two cakes inside, and dust the top with sifted icing sugar. Reserve any leftover chocolate spread for another use.

Chocolate Biscuit Cake

This is one of the most sumptuous, sinful chocolate recipes you will ever find. To compound what is undoubtedly a prime example of the Sin of Gluttony, the mixture can also be used as a filling for the Starfruit and Almond Tarts on page 180.

Any leftover mixture from this recipe can be made into Chocolate Almond Balls (see variation below right).

To make the Dark Chocolate Spread, break the chocolate in a heat-proof bowl and melt over a pan of hot water, stirring.

Pour the Egg Sauce Base into a bowl, add the sugar and mix until dissolved. Mix in the eggs and the melted chocolate.

To make the cake, first grease two large 19 cm/7½ inch cake tins and base line with non-stick baking paper.

Make the Sugar Syrup Sauce Base according to the method on page 156, then add the extra sugar and mix until dissolved. Beat the eggs then stir them into the mixture, together with the melted chocolate.

Divide the mixture equally between two bowls. Add the ground almonds and flour to one of the bowls and mix well.

Spread the mixture over the base of each tin.

Bake in a preheated oven at 180°C (350°F) Gas Mark 4 for about 40 minutes, until beginning to darken all over. Remove and allow to cool until crisp. Spread one base with a thick layer of Dark Chocolate Spread, and the other with White Chocolate Spread (recipe opposite). Reserve any leftover chocolate spreads for another use.

Gently place one iced cake on top of the other, with the two iced surfaces together. Dust the top with an icing sugar pattern and cool.

300 ml/½ pint
Sugar Syrup Sauce Base

250 g/8 oz sugar

2 eggs

200 g/7 oz good-quality chocolate, such as Menier, melted

125 g/4 oz ground almonds

20 g/¾ oz plain flour

White Chocolate Spread
(see recipe opposite)

sifted icing sugar, for dusting

For the dark chocolate spread:
200 g/7 oz good-quality cooking chocolate, such as Menier

300 ml/½ pint Egg Sauce Base
(see page 14)

250 g/8 oz caster sugar

2 egg

Alternatively:
CHOCOLATE
ALMOND BALLS
Dampen the palms of your hands with water, and roll the mixture into balls. Allow to dry before serving. We also like them rolled in cocoa or dessicated coconut.

Index